The Pharisees Among Us

by

Warnell Roberson

Enjoy The READ AND
MAY God Continue To
BLess you

RoseDog 🐾 Books

PITTSBURGH, PENNSYLVANIA 15222

RoseDog Books
701 Smithfield Street
Pittsburgh, PA 15222
Visit our website at *www.rosedogbookstore.com*

ISBN: 978-1-4349-7291-0
eISBN: 978-1-4349-1929-8

THE PHARISEES AMONG US

Why has the bible, being one of the most read books in the world for thousands of years, has for that same period of time, separated us by race, by gender and by religion? This is a compelling book, a book which delivers an equally compelling message........Truly, an inspiring read for those who believe, an enlightening read for those who do not!

WRITTEN BY
WARNELL ROBERSON
author of
"CAN YOU SEE WHAT I SEE"

PART ONE

STRATEGY NUMBER ONE OF GOD'S OVERALL PLAN

Before God had destroyed the world with a flood He realized that unlike with Adam and Eve, the new people that would occupy His new world would need leadership and teaching. So, Noah and his family were saved and was told to go forth, be fruitful and multiply. It is from this command that the Prophets came forth, along with Abraham, Isaac, Jacob, Moses and Joshua, all of whom had the responsibility of leading as well as teaching God's chosen people. Part one of this book will deal with God' first strategy.........

Section One

"400 Years of Our People," by Michael Escoffery. Mixed media 1994–1995. Art Resource, New York, NY

PREFACE

This is a story about the bible, and yes the complete bible, both the Old Testament as well as the New Testament. It is a story about God's direct interactions with man through the establishment of a new society of His chosen people, it is a story about God's introduction of ten laws given to one man. Continuing, it is a story about the coming of Jesus Christ and His direct interactions with man through His teaching of grace, truth and forgiveness to a different generation of God's chosen people.

This is a story about God's words. And, last but not least, this is a story about the refusal of some to accept Jesus Christ as the one and only Son of God, compared to others that did accept Jesus Christ as the Son of God and Savior of the world.

In John 1:17, John testified before the Priest and Levites that were sent by the Jews in Jerusalem, stating: "For the laws were given to you by Moses; grace and truth came through Jesus Christ." It was this testimony by John, who was also Jewish and a relative of Jesus, that so clearly Illustrated the two theologies that were and are practiced as a result of the Old and New Testaments.

Understanding that the Bible remains one of the most popular, most read books in the world, yet, it is difficult to understand how for so long this book that was written about God and the Son of God still, to this day, separates us by race, by religion and by gender. So, I decided that in order for me to bring to you the story of these long standing divides, I had to first of all prepare myself with the necessary wisdom. To accomplish this, I set as an objective to learn more about what is contained in the Bible.

My strategy was to read, analyze and study at least three or more books in the Bible each week. During my efforts I discovered one very important fact, and that is, the Bible does contain God's words, however, these same words were interpreted and recorded by none other than God's own creation, and that happens to be man (the male) himself. So, as I studied the Bible, I continually reminded myself that unlike God, man was not at that time, and is not currently, infallible. As a result, when I ran into verses that contradicted each other, in order to gain a better perspective of exactly what was being presented, I moved my study from the Bible and sought out a more coherent explanation on the same subject matter, during the same time in history but is contained in other religious narratives, or in many cases, I used my God given common sense. After all God has given us all the gifts of The Holy Spirit to inspire and direct our common sense, while at the same time, it drives our need for knowledge. Nevertheless, God leaves the choice up to us to pursue and use these two important gifts. My dear friends, I have accepted this soul saving challenge.

One should also understand that as Christians, understanding the bible goes hand and hand with understanding the messages contained in the bible; then utilizing our God given wisdom, we should apply the appropriate messages to our lives by way of our behavior. So, it is because of the fallible nature of man's understanding, I've included in my study of the bible many other books written about religion in order that I may present to you a broader perspective surrounding both the Old and New Testaments.

It should be said at this point that no one has an all encompassing knowledge about what is presented in the bible, including me. So prior to writing this book, I ask God to grant me the wisdom to do the very best that I could, utilizing the reasoning power and common sense that He has given me. And, I must say at this point, that even though the extra research that I conducted took me outside the contents of the bible, and actually slowed my writing progress on this book, I have, on the other hand, truly enjoyed the blessing of knowledge that God has allowed me to acquire, not only for the purpose of this book, but for the purpose of living my life.

So now that I have completed the necessary research, I now feel that I understand why some religions that are practiced by some advocate the theology that is presented in The Old Testament, while there are still others that practiced the theology that is presented in The New Testament. But I must say that regardless of where one's beliefs and subsequent practices rest in the bible, such biblical separation was never God's will for His plan (the bible) to be limited to one book of the bible or the other; No, from what I have discovered, the bible is one plan by God, consisting of two parts, both of which should be incorporated into our lives if we are to understand where we come from, why we are here and why we have the free will to dictate where it is we will spend our eternal lives.

In writing this book, it is my intention to assist those who seek the assistance to better understand both sections of the bible, and with such knowledge hopefully we will better comprehend not only God's total plan, but most importantly, our ACCOUNTABILITY under His plan.

Still other areas emerge that challenge my comprehension, for example, I discovered that part of the reason for many people's biblical separation and lack of understanding, rest in their inability to come to terms with two issues: Edifications in the bible and Interpretations of what is said in the bible, as well as the fact that both The Old Testament and The New Testament were inspired by men from the same Jewish Faith, but two theologies were advocated, Judaism and Christianity.

Also, in The Old Testament God was accountable for guiding and directing mankind. As a result, we see God interacting with Abraham and his wife Sarah, selecting them to be the father and mother of us all. Then we see God select Moses, who was born Jewish but raised by an Egyptian mother; God changed and redirected his life, then dispatched him back to Egypt to deliver His people from four hundred years of bondage, and all during that time, it was God that maintained direct contact with Moses.

Moses was given ten laws by God, and in return he presented these laws to God's chosen people.

It was these laws that were carried on to the Promise Land by Joshua, then they were passed on to the Kingship of David, and from David to the Prophets, on to the Psalmist and the Writers of Wisdom, right on down to the Pharisees. By this time the laws had expanded to over six hundred, and it was the belief that these laws and decrees was the real conduit to God. However, when we compare this theology to the theology in The New Testament, we find that a new theology arrives with the introduction of God only Son, Jesus Christ. You see, Jesus Christ proclaimed that the only path to God was through the belief in Him as the only Son of God, and it would be God's Grace through Him and His forgiveness that would propel mankind to his planned salvation. I must admit upfront, that as a result of my study and research, what is very clear is that whenever mankind sought salvation directly from God and not His Son Jesus Christ, Man's efforts failed!

The Pharisees during ancient times, just like many of us in the world today were guilty of such misjudgments. It is however difficult to understand the Pharisees lack of faith when compared to ours, because we are suppose to live by faith and not sight, nevertheless the Pharisees had the sights and they witness all of the miracules performed by Jesus, so we know that they knew. Also there was a Pharisee by the name of Nicodemus who visited with Jesus late at night so as not to be seen and he said to Jesus: "Rabbi, we know that you are a teacher that comes from God, for no one could perform the miraculous signs that you are doing if God was not with him." When we examine Nicodemus' statement to Jesus, we see that the telling phrase was, WE KNOW. He did not say that I know, but, WE KNOW. This clearly indicated that Nicodemus was speaking not of his personal knowledge of Jesus' true identity, but the awareness of the Pharisees as a group. So yes we know that the Pharisees were very much aware. The message that we as Christians should take away from The Pharisees Among Us is this: Don't confuse keeping the laws that manage our civil discourse, protect our properties, demand cleanliness of our bodies and eating certain foods, while not eating others as our conduits to Heaven; for such laws only govern our lives while on this earth. Now let's not forget Paul, the Jewish Pharisee who was converted to Christianity; in his letter to the Galatains he wrote: "For if a law had been given that could give life, then righteousness would certainly come by the law." Here Paul's message tells us two things: 1. We should read and study the bible making sure that we understand what we read and fully comprehend the relationship between The Old Testament and The New Testament, in that both books represents God's total plan. 2. We must learn to identify the pharisaical hypocrisy that still exist right here in our world today in order that we do not allow such hypocrisy to come into our hearts and replace our faith in Jesus Christ. It is this daily effort by the way, that presents the day to day struggles to right the wrongs that we do to ourselves as well as others;

SCRIPTURE REFERENCES AND BACKGROUND INFORMATION TAKEN FROM THE FOLLOWING BIBLES:

The African American Jubilee Edition, King James version March, 1999

The Spiritual Formation Bible Edition, New International Version. Copyright 1999 by Zondervan Corporation.

OTHER BOOKS OF REFERENCE

* *

The Jewish Contemporaries of Jesus (Pharisees, Sadducees & Esseness) By Gunter Stemberger, first published in English by Fortress Press, 1995

Pictures of the Black Pharaohs of Ancient Egypt and the Statues of the Nubian Kings, taken from The National Geographic Magazine

February, 2008

DEDICATION

This book is dedicated to my three grand children, Kaescha, Austin and Hunter.

    May they always understand that being of mix race, they too share in the blessed common bond of all of God's people that preceded them in this historical book that guide our Christian lives; the Holy Bible.

INTRODUCTION

During the time that Jesus walked and taught on this earth, there existed three schools of Judasim that were contemporaries at that time. These contemporaries were: The Pharisees, The Sadducees and The Essenes. Of these three branches of Judaism, The Pharisees, because of their power, had the most interaction with Jesus Christ during the short period of time that He spent preaching and teaching on this earth.

As such, it was the Pharisees that played the most significant role in the movement against Jesus and the theology that He advocated.

Also, because of their religious and social powers, combined with their influence with the Roman government, the Pharisees controlled the lives of the Jewish people, by making sure that the over six hundred laws were adhered to. And, when they thought that their powers were threaten, they would exercise their influence with the Roman government to expel such threats in the name of their religious laws or the Roman rules that govern their society at the time.

And so it was when Jesus started on His mission to teach and preach to the people, both Jews and Gentiles, exposing them to the message that His Father in Heaven had sent Him to teach, the Pharisees, first of all, didn't believe that He was the Son of God, and secondly, they believed that what He was teaching and preaching conflicted with the laws that had been handed down from Moses. So the stage was set, and it was upon this stage that the collision course between Jesus Christ, the only Son of God and the Pharisees, leaders of the then Jewish Nation was set for history to record. This collision course was a powerful one and it clearly defined the difference between the struggling early lawless world which is covered in the Old Testament, where as in the New Testament, the world has grown rapidly and by the time that Jesus taught and preached, there were laws and decrees in place to control the society.

Now, even though there were laws that controlled the society, still a new form of religion arrived with the presence of Jesus Christ, a religion that did not emphasize laws and decrees, although respect for the laws were advocated, nevertheless, the new emphasis would be placed on one's eternal life, which would be through Jesus Christ, the Son of God, and not the laws that God gave to Moses. Living one's life with faith in Jesus Christ, as the one and only Son of God would be mankind's only way to heaven.

Also, love and forgiveness would play a major role in the religion that Christ would preach and, most importantly, Jesus' messages would be open to all people, Jews as well as Gentiles alike, therefore fulfilling God's promise that he made to Abraham that all nations will be brought under him as their worldly father.

In Paul's letter to the Galatians which is found in chapter 3 verse 19, he asked the question, what was the purpose of the law? And Paul answered his own question by saying this: "The law was added because of the transgressing by the people until Abraham's seed had come as per God's promise." Paul continued on in verse 21 and 22, by asking still another question, that being: "Is the law therefore opposed to the promise that was made to Abraham?" Again, Paul answered by saying: "Absolutely not, for if a law could have been given that could give life, then righteousness would have certainly come by the law." Paul's letter to the Galatians continued with him writing that the scriptures declares that the whole world is a prisoner of sin, so the saving grace that was promised to Abraham, will come to those who believe through their faith in Jesus Christ.

So, on and on, I continued with my research, and as my reading of the bible, as well as other books written about the world's religious activities progressed, my thoughts as well as what I was reading started to move at the same time toward a single conclusion, and that was, regardless of the Old Testament's teachings or the New Testament's teachings, The Holy Spirit was telling me that God had only one plan which consist of two strategies and these two strategies was intended to benefit not only the Jewish people but the Gentiles as well. So, as our book begins I will start in the book of Exodus. It is here that we find that Moses and the Twelve Tribes of Israel have departed from their four hundred years of bondage in Egypt and they have crossed the Red Sea. But, as many may know, or may not know, Moses and the Children of Israel were made to wander around in the desert for some forty years. So, it is at this point that I will attempt to start this story by explaining their long, hard, nomadic journey.

For some four hundred years, the Israelites had been enslaved, and just like the many thousands of their Africans brothers that were also enslaved thousands of years after them, when the Israelites freedom finally came and they were released, their bodies enjoyed the immeadiate freedom, however because of the adverse effects that slavery has on one's mind, it was therefore their minds that remained in captivity. Nevertheless, from my view of history, this is where the correlation between the Jewish slaves and the Africans slaves must and should end because when one study the mind-set of the African slave compared to the Jewish slave's mind-set, one will discover the difference. You see the Africans were captured in their own country, exported thousands of miles to the Western World where they were sold to the highest bidders which split up their families, they were then made to breed like animals, after which the females were raped repeatedly by their new masters or the associates of their masters; taught that their hard, back breaking work should only benefit their masters, they were, as a result, deprived of an education which would benefit them and when they tried to escape to God knows where, they were beaten with whips, or one half of a foot was cut off. It was these types of battle scars that spoke to the African's desire for freedom. And it was the spiritual songs that emanated from their back breaking field work that tells us even today about their strong constant faith, a faith not in a promise land, but in the eternal salvation of that man that they kept hearing talk about, a man by the name of Jesus Christ. Now to make my point, let's contrast this with the Israelites' faith, which was time after time in our story proven to be extremely limited and restricted only to what they could see and touch. Also, the Children of Israel were used to being told exactly what to do. They In turn exhibited no skills with which to take care of themselves; so, at the time, their ability to manage a Promise Land of Milk and Honey that God had promised them was, at the time, out of the question. As a result of all of these man-made flaws, the Children of Israel repeatedly sinned against God who had freed them. So it was God's plan that this particular Jewish generation that He had freed from Egypt, be delayed for some forty years. In doing so, God would then allow adequate time for the training of a new generation of The Twelve Tribes of Israel to take place, which by the way would still be Moses' accountability. After the training of a new generation had taken place, as well as laws and decrees implemented with consequences to follow, as along with the slave mentality that existed eradicated, God would then allow a new generation of The Twelve Tribes of Israel to enter the land that was promised to their father Abraham.

We enter our story at the point where Moses has successfully departed from the land of Egypt, and leading the Israelites, they have embarked on a journey that should have taken some ten days, but because of the Israelites sinful ways and God's plan, the trip would take some forty years.

On this journey the Lord was leading them by placing a cloud that was shaped like a pillar of stone to guide them on their way, and by night God supplied a pillar of fire which gave them light. This allowed them to travel by day or night. Not too long after they had departed Egypt, the Lord said to Moses, "tell the Israelites to turn around and go back and camp by the Red Sea. Pharoah will then think that they are lost and wandering around in circles in a state of confusion." God then said to Moses that He would harden Pharoah's heart and this would make him pursue them, and when he does, I will gain glory for myself through Pharoah and his armies, then the Egyptians will know that I am the Lord!

And so it was, when Pharoah and his armies was approching and the Israelites saw them, they became extremely terrified and they cried out to the Lord, while directing their cry to Moses saying, "was it because there were no graves in Egypt that you brought us to the desert to die? Moses answered them saying," stand still and you will see the deliverance the Lord will bring to you today. For the Egyptians that you see today, you will never see again. The Lord will fight for you, you need only stand still." With that statement by Moses, he then raised his staff and the Red Sea was split apart and was kept apart by a vary strong wind which started blowing east, and as the Israelites started crossing the Red Sea, they were able to do so on dry land, traversing between two exyremely high walls of sea water. And, after the Israelites had completed their crossing, the Egyptians, seeing this divine opening, started to enter onto this dry path of land with their horse driven chariots and marching foot soliers, but when they started their move the strong east wind stopped blowing and the high walls of sea water came roaring back into place and in the process, every Egyptian soldier and horse driven chariot that had tryed to cross was drowned.

Now when the Israelites saw the great power of God displayed against the Egyptians they feared God and His power, and for the time being they would put their faith and trust in Him and His servant, Moses.

Well, after such an awesome display of power, you would think that no more miracles by God would be needed to maintain the Israelites' faith, right? Well, think again, remember, the Israelites are physically free but their faith was still based on exactly what they could touch and see, which means that as future tribulations mounted, more of their faith would be needed for each hardship. So, lets continue on with their forty year journey.

Moses and the children of Israel continued following the cloud that God was leading them with, and in doing so, they headed away from the Red Sea and toward the desert of Shur. When they had travel for some three days without water, and when they came to a place called Marah, they found water but they could not drink it because the water was bitter. So once again the people complain to Moses, saying, "what are we to drink." Moses in turn cried out to the Lord and the Lord directed him to a piece of wood. Moses threw the piece of wood onto the water and the water became sweet. But after this outcry by the Israelites' God laid out a test for them by establishing a law and a decree. God said; "if you listen closely to the word of God and do what is right in His eyes, if you pay attention to His commands and keep all of His decrees, I will not bring on you the diseases that I brought on the Egyptians; for I am the Lord that heals you." Well, after hearing this from the Lord, Moses felt that enough had been said, so he continued to lead the Israelites on to a place called Elim. It was in Elim that they found twelve springs of water and palm trees, so they drank and they rested. When they left Elim they went forward to a place called the Desert of Sin, which is between Elim and Sinai. The trip by this time had lasted some forty five days. But even after God had evoked His law and decree, the Israelites had no sooner arrived when they started their faithless complaining against Moses and his brother Aaron, shouting," if only we had died by the Lord's hand in Egypt! because there we sat around pots of meat and ate all of the food that we wanted, but you, you have brought us out into this desert to starve all of us to death." So once again a miracle was in store for them. The Lord said to Moses that He would rain down bread from heaven for them. Then God instructed Moses that the people should go out each day and gather up enough food for that day. But God also told Moses that on this day I will test them and see whether they will follow my instructions. Now, allow me to say at this point that in my corporate training I know that a plan must have three important points and they are: 1). An objective, 2). It must have assigned accountabilities and 3). It must have strategies or actions steps. God has already assigned His objective, that being: TO REINTRODUCE MANKIND'S ETERNAL SALVATION VIA MANKIND'S OWN FREE WILL. Also, He has assigned the accountabilities as well, however in The Old Testament He has assigned the accountabilities unto Himself because God is working DIRECTLY with the principles in The Old Testament to carry out the strategies assigned. I will highlight this point again at the appropriate time in part two of this book. For now let's return to the story where God Is giving instructions which will test the Israelites. The instructions that God gave to Moses are as follows: On the sixth day the Israelites are to prepare what they bring in, and that should be twice as much as they bring in on other days. So Moses told Aaron to gather up the entire community and tell them to come before the Lord, because He has heard their grumbling. While Aaron was speaking collectively to the Israelites, they looked toward the desert and there on the horizon they saw the glory of the Lord appearing in a cloud. As they were staring at the cloud, the Lord spoke to Moses saying: "I have heard the grumbling of the Israelites. Tell them at twilight they will eat meat and in the morning they will be filled with bread. Then they will know that I am the Lord their God." So now we see that God will test the faith of the Israelites, and, just as so many times before the slave minded Israelites will fail the test. Nevertheless, God in all of His mercy will continue to provide for them. And so, this journey of the Israelites continued moving from place to place as directed by God himself.

Yet they were stopped again, this time at a place called Rephidim, and, just like so many places that they had ventured through, there was no water to drink; so again as they had so many other times, the children of Israel started complaining and this time the complaints were directed straight to Moses. They shouted, "Why did you bring us out of Egypt to make us and our children and our livestock die of thrist?" Now hearing this, Moses became extremely frustrated and he expelled his frustrations in a angry outburst directed at the Lord, right in front of the Israelites. With this outburst, Moses' journey to the Promise Land, at that very moment had come to an end, but not the forty year journey for which the Lord had chosen him and, subsequently, was still holding him accountable for leading and managing.

And so now the glory of God rained down on the children of Israel, supplying them with bread in the mornings, which the Israelites called Manna, and in the evenings quail would cover the camp ground, supplying them with an abundance of meat. Yes the Lord in all of His glorious splender, continued to work His miracles for His chosen people; and yet His chosen people still were unable to understand that their almighty God could do anything, yes anything, but fail.

While Moses and the Israelites were still in Rephidim, they were attacked by the Amalekites, so Moses instructed Joshua to choose some men from the community and go out to fight the Amalekites. And, while you are fighting I will stand on top of the hill with my staff of God in my hands. But as Moses stood on the hill with his arms raised above his head, his arms became tired and he had to lower them, when this happened, the Amalekites would start to win the battle against Joshua. Seeing this, both Aaron and Hur rushed to the side of Moses, and as they stood on either side, they lifted Moses' arms and held them above his head until sunset. With God's staff raised high, Joshua was able to defeat the Amalekites. Before moving on with this story, I must at this point, give some perspective to what is about to happen next. You see Moses had killed a man in Egypt so he ran away in order to escape Pharoah's law. Moses crossed the desert and settle in Midian. He worked as a shepperd for a priest named Jethro and while working for Jethro, Moses met and married Jethro's daughter Zepporah, they were married and they had two children. For fourteen years Moses worked as a shepperd before God dispatched him back to Egypt to free the Israelites. Before leaving, Moses sent his wife and children to stay with his wife's father. Now, while leading the children of Israel out of Egypt, the trip had taken him back into the desert, and Jethro, hearing of his return came out to meet him at the Mount of God and he brought along with him Moses' wife and two children. When Moses' family arrived, Moses greeted his father in law and invited him into his tent. There, Moses told Jethro all about the things that God had done to Pharoah and the Egyptians. Then Jethro, who was the Priest of Midian and a true beliveer in God, offered up a burnt offering and other sacrifices to God. Joining them at the time were Aaron and the other elders of Israel, who had come to eat bread with Moses' father-in-law in the presence of God. The next day moses returned to his duties as Judge, and the people were around him from morning until evening. When Moses father-in-law saw all of what he was doing for the people, he cautioned Moses about becoming too over worked and still the people were not getting satisfied. Moses' answer to his father-in-law was that the people came to him seeking God's will. So, when ever they had disputes they are brought to me and I decide between the parties by informing them of God's laws and decrees. Jethro then explained to Moses that the way that he was preforming the duties of Judge was just too hard and if he continued, both he and the people would wear themselves out. At that point, Jethro gave Moses some very sound advice by telling him that he should be the representative of the people before God and Bring their disputes to him. Jethro continued by telling Moses that he should teach the people the laws and decrees and show them how they should live and the duties they were to perform. Also, he should select capable men to represent the Twelve Tribes of Israel, men who fear God and hate dishonest gain; he should then appoint these men over thousands, over hundreds, over fifties, over twenties and over tens. Then he should have them serve as full time judges for the respective group that they represent. However, these representatives should bring only the most difficult cases to him. Now if he did this and God so commands, he would then be able to with stand the strain, and most importantly, all of the people would be attended to in a timely manner, and as a result, all of the people will go away satisfied.

Moses did exactly as his father-in-law had instructed and much to his surprise he found that his new management style of delegating authority worked extremely well. So, after Jethro had made his contribution to his son-in-law Moses, he departed back to his home in Midian. And now with his departure, I will admit to you that the real reason that I interjected this information about Moses' father-in-law was to try and correct the negative mind-sets of some African Americans as, well as some White Americans that people from Africa are not even in the Bible due to the curse that was to have been placed on Ham, the second son of Noah. It has been exactly this type of mind-set over the years, which I might add is due mainly to geographical ignorance, or a lack of a proper education about such matters, or just plain racism, or maybe it's all three that have cause the racial separation mentioned in the beginning of this book. In any event, because such information remains mostly dormant in our societies, both African Americans and White Americans have, as a result, been kept basically ignorant about race in the Bible. This and this alone, in our day and time, has been a major contributor to the separation of God's people by race and race alone. However, I must make one thing perfectly clear and that is the Bible is not, and should not ever become a book about race, but at the same time the knowledge about the different races in the Bible should not be consciously or unconsciously suppressed. That is why when one read and study the Bible, one should understand what one is reading about, who one is reading about and most importantly, where the events that one reads about took place. It is because such information does not freely emanate from our institutions and pulpits, that I will take this opportunity to further explore what many of our so called leaders today should be including in their communications and curriculums, and that is the accurate description of people of color in the Bible.

I will start with Moses' father-in-law, Jethro (also called Reuel). It is worth noting from the start that one of the first countries that is mentioned in the first book of the Bible, (Genesis), is Ethiopia. At the time however, Ethiopia was known as the Land of Cush. Also in this first book of the Bible, we find that creation itself is introduced. Now since Ethiopia/the Land of Cush is introduced in the beginning of the Bible, and this land was, and still is located in the costal Northeast area of Africa, then common sense compels us to believe that creation and the Garden of Eden was located in Africa. The Bible also tells us that Jethro was of African descent, in that he was a descendent of Ham, being that he was Cush's son, and Cush was the first son of Ham. Cush founded Ethiopia. So Jethro, being the son of Cush was Ethiopian, but like so many other people during that time, he migrated from his family and settled in Midian where he became a priest. To fully understand how the Ethiopians looked at that time and still do today, one must be guided by history's description. You see their description is derived from two Greek words, which are: ETHIOS, which means "Burned" and OPES, which means "FACE." This description of the Ethiopians clearly indicates their true skin color. Following this same genealogy, Zepporah, who was the daughter of Jethro and the wife of Moses, would have also been a person of color. Now if we pause right here in our story and examine exactly what has taken place in our ancient history, we will see clearly that it was an African Priest from Ethiopia who lived in Midian that was instrumental in getting Moses managerially organized so that he could better perform the duties that God had placed upon him and, as a result, God was still holding him accountable for implementing.

Also, Africans in the Bible closely interacted with other biblical people that are so well known to us today by their names as well as their race, including Jesus himself. But the African people in the Bible are known only by their names or their genders but not by their race. So now that we are aware that Jethro was of African descent, one can now start to measure their African ancestors' contribution during biblical times by the actions of Jethro, because without his experience and knowledge of leadership, which he shared with God's servant Moses, Moses would have continued experiencing extreme hardship in the performance of the duties that had been placed upon him by God. And, without this improvement in Moses' management style, the Children of Israel's forty year nomadic journey would have been much more difficult, if not longer. It is this type of knowledge for hundreds of years that have for whatever reason (3) have remained void in too many of our educational and religious institutions as well as remaining dormant in the minds of many of our leading clergy and scholars that represents these institutions in question. So today when we look at the ignorance that still exist about people of color in the Bible by the majority of God's people, one must ask the very obvious question, and that is: Exactly Who Are The Pharisees That Are Among Us?

Before bringing to a close this prospective which started with Moses' father-in-law, I must also insert this note about the God that I know and worship; you see, in all of the research work that I conducted while writing this book, I never discovered at any time that God ever made a mistake when he spoke. What I did discover however was that God was always extremely specific. For example, God told Noah exactly what type of wood to use on the ark, Noah was given the height, the width and length of the ark. God gave Noah the proper instructions on the type of windows and doors to be used. Noah was told what type of animals to bring on board, even the sex of the animals along with the type of food that they would need. God then specifically told Noah to board the ark with his wife, his three sons, Shem, Ham, Japheth and their wives. Now, it is at this point that if Canaan had been present and the son of Ham, then God actually omitted Canaan; as a matter of fact, God never mentions Canaan either as Ham's son or Noah's grandson when instructions to board or exit the ark was given. Now I think that we can all agree that God did not make a mistake, so my God given common sense tells me that the real reason that God did not mention Canaan was for the simple reason that Canaan was not there. So I will attempt to interject the presence of Canaan when and where I feel his presence belongs.

Let's look at Genesis, 8:20, it states: And Noah began to be a husband (to me this was the author's way of saying that Noah had sex with his wife and begot Canaan, because Noah was already a husband) and he planted a vineyard. This verse went on to say that Noah worked the soil and planted a vineyard; now working the soil and then planting the vineyard would have, in itself, taken some time, then the grapes had to grow and mature, then harvesting the grapes had to take place as well as processing for the juice. The wine would then have to be bottled and stored in order for the wine to achieve it's intoxicating properties. In any event, for all of this to have taken place, it would have taken several years, which was enough time for Noah's youngest son Canaan to have grown up. So when Noah drank the first fruits of his labor, he became drunk and fell asleep. When he awoke from his drunken sleep and knew what his youngest son had done to him he said "Curse Be To Canaan; remember, one must understand that up until this point Japheth had been mentioned over and over in the scriptures of Genesis as Noah's youngest son. At no time in these verses did Noah ever curse Ham, so how could he have been cursed, plus, God had already blessed all three of Noah's sons, Shem, Ham and Japheth and their wives, and a covenant was made with them when they left the ark. So why, you may ask, was Canaan ever described as the son of Ham, with this edited phrase, (And Ham was the father of Canaan) and for what purpose was it done?

Well now, allow me to start off by saying that the reason was not purposeful, in that the author (s) had no inclanations to promote the idea that Africans, being black and descendents of Ham were cursed. Instead their reasoning centered around the relations between the Israelites, the Canaanites and the Philistines that lived in the land of Canaan. You see by this time the Canaanites had assimilated and were not full blood African people, but Semites and Indo-Europeans who lived in Palestine. So the purpose of the author (s) had nothing to do with Ham and his black descendents being cursed. On the other hand however, with the focus placed on Ham, it did helped established the very popular conclusion that Ham was cursed, and that made it possible for racists people to use Genesis 9:18-29 as their theological justification for the oppression of African people and their descendents, African Americans. One should keep in mind however, that the idea of Ham being cursed is not the fault of the Bible. But it does reflect a severe lack of knowledge of biblical scholarship. Also, one should keep in mind that when the curse was placed on Canaan, it was because of his behavior, and not his race.

FOLLOWING ARE HISTORICAL, PICTURES AND BACKGROUND INFORMATION <u>ALONG</u> WITH TERROTORIES OF AFRICAN PEOPLE IN THE BIBLE

1. Egypt, which is also called Mizraim, meaning red mud. Mizraim was also the name of Ham's Son, and it was Mizraim who founded Egypt. The Egyptian society contributed much to the civilization of their time. And it was in Egypt that Joseph, Mary and the Baby Jesus took refuge among people of color in order to escape the killing of all first born babies by order of King Herod. It is important to note that the skin color of the Hebrew people during biblical times was of a darker hue than the Hebrews of today; the skin color of today's Hebrews came about as a result of racial assimilation, just as the Africans who were brought to the Western World during the slave trade were dark skin people, and through mixing with other races, they too became lighter in skin color; THERE WERE NO HIGH YELLOW AFRICANS BROUGHT TO THE WESTERN WORLD AS SLAVES, nevertheless many of their descendents as a result of race mixing do currently have much lighter skin complexions today.

2. Libia, located west of Egypt along the northern coast of Africa, was founded by Put, another son of Ham. This society specialized in producing mercenaries who fought for other countries; they were great warriors.

3. Ethiopia, derives it's name from the Greek language and has the following meanings: Ethios (meaning burned) and Opes (meaning face). This description speaks to the fact that the Ethiopians were, and still are, a dark race of people. Also in Genesis 2:13, it states that one of the rivers that waters the Garden of Eden was the Gihon, which flows through the entire Land of Cush (Ethiopia). It is for this reason that many argue that the Garden of Eden was in Africa.

4. The Land of Canaan and Hebron was founded by Canaan, remember him, he was the one identified by Noah as his youngest son that sinned against him. Well, this society was extremely advanced technology wise and they perfected the manufacturing of the feared chariot.

5. Jebus, now called Jerusalem, here the inhabitants were Called Jebusites, they too were the descendents of Canaan, therefore, the first Hebrews to occupy Jerusalem were of African descent.

6. The Land of Shinar, which is called Sumer in the Hebrew Text, this was the place where God confused the people's language, and, as a result, this city is called The City of Babal. Shinar was founded by Nimrod, the son of Cush. The people that lived in Shinar were described as SWARTY (meaning black) and, they had a very high degree of intelligence. These people were known as Sumaritians. Remember the woman that Jesus went out of His way to meet and speak with at the well, was also Sumaritian. Also, it is important to note that in John 8: 48, the Pharisees thought that Jesus was a Sumaritian, now it would be hard for them to make such a comparison if Jesus' color and facial features were that of a Caucasian.

Before I depart from this background information on African people and their respective territories, I want to make a point about Canaan's sin against Noah, you know, the point about the Authors (s) being too sensitive about what their culture should and should not hear.

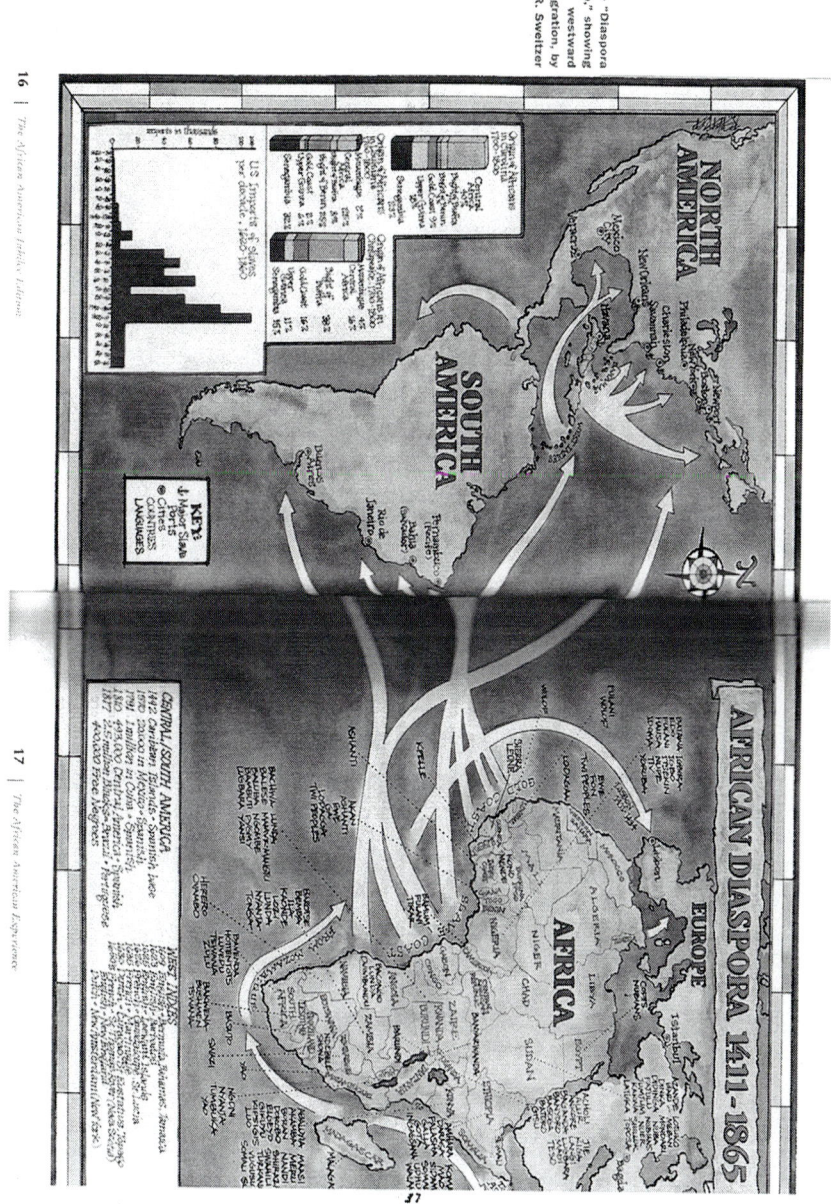

Well, allow me to elaborate about my feeling in this area. To do this we must go back to Canaan. Canaan, as per Noah's claim was his youngest son. Now allow me to give you the names of Canaan's descendents: Canaan you see was the father of Sidom, his first born, and of the Hittites, the Jebusites, the Amorites, the Girgashites, the Hivites, the Arkites, the Sinites, the Arvadites, the Zemarites and the Hamathites. These were the clans of Canaan. However, as time progressed, the Canaanite Clans because of their growing numbers, needed more land, this in turn caused their boarders to grow in such a way so as to cover the territories from Sidom, named after Canaan's first born, to Gerar as far as Gaza, and then toward Sodom, Gomorrah, Admah and Zeboiim, as far as Lasha. Well, when God was going to destroy both Sodom and Gomorrah, He sent two Angles to tell Lot to take his wife and his two daughters and leave Sodom. So while the Angles were inside of Lot's home talking with him, lets examine what happened; we can do this by looking at Genesis 19-4-9; these verses tells us that before they had gone to bed, all of the men from every part of the city of Sodom, both the young and the old surrounded Lot's house. They then called to Lot, "Where are the men who came to visit you tonight? Bring them out to us so that we can have sex with them." Lot, hearing this went outside to meet with them, as he did, he shut the door behind him and said, "No, my friends. Don't do this wicked thing. Look, I have two daughters who have never slept with a man. Let me bring them out to you, and you can do what you like with them. But don't do anything to these Men, for they have come under the protection of my roof."

"Get out of our way" they replied. Then they said, "This fellow came here as an alien, and now he wants to play the Judge? We'll treat you worse than them." They kept bringing the pressure on Lot and moved forward to break down the door.

It would appear, after reading these verses, that the Canaanites, because of the curse placed on Canaan by Noah himself, were genetically pre-disposed to this MAN on MAN sexual behavior, and, since the men that showed up at Lot's home consisted of both the young and the old, it would also appear that the curse placed on Canaan was generational, which would coincide with the impact that curses had during biblical times. This now explains what Canaan, the patriarch of the Canaanites sin actually was against Noah, and it also tell us that the curse placed at the time, was simply passed on generationally to Canaan's descendents as others curses in the bible have been historically. As such, this would then explain certainly more realisticly, that whatever happened between Canaan and Noah was sexual, and this version would then historically coincides with the generational impact of such curses at that time.

However, the recording in the bible of Noah waking up and knowing, without any evidence what Canaan had done to him, to me represents yet another culturally sensitive area that was rearranged for the benefit of the readers and the then evolving church. In returning to our story, we find that the Children of Israel are three months out in their nomadic journey to the Promise Land, and they have made camp in the desert, located in fornt of

Mount Sinai. Moses went upon the mountain to meet and converse with God, and God spoke with Moses telling him to go back down the mountain and tell the Israelites the following: You have seen what I did to Egypt and how I carried you on eagles' wings and brought you to myself. Now if you obey me fully and keep my covenant, then out of all nations you will be my treasured possession. God continued, although the whole world is mine, you will be for me a kingdom of Priests and a Holy Nation. God said to Moses, this is what you should speak to the Israelites. Now, what God was really telling Moses was that His selection of the Jewish people would not come without their spiritual responsibility, in that their religion and their society should serve as a shining example for the rest of the world to follow. Moses as instructed, departed down the mountain and called all of the elders of the people and told them all of the things that God had told him to speak, and the elders all responded together saying "We will do everything the Lord has said." So Moses took their answer back to the Lord. God then told Moses that He would come to him in a dense cloud, so that the people will hear me talking to you and they will always place their trust in you. Then God said to Moses, go back down to the people and consecrate them today and tomorrow. You should have them wash their clothes and they should be ready on the third day, because it is on that day that I will decend on Mount Sinai in sight of all the people. On that third day there was thounder and lighting, with a thick cloud over Mount Sinai, everybody in the camp trembled. Then Moses led the people out of camp to meet with God. Moses spoke and the voice of God answered him; these are the words that God spoke: I am the Lord your God who brought you out of Egypt, out of the land of slavery. You should have no other god before me. You should not make idols for yourself that are in the form of anything in Heaven above, or on earth below or in the waters beneath; For the Lord your God is a jeallous God. It is at this point that I must pause and ask you to consider this second commandment that was just given to the Children of Israel, the one about idol gods; you see for hundreds of years mankind have created distorted art forms depicting both God the Father, who no one has ever seen, including Moses, and Jesus Christ, who historically has been seen. In doing so, mankind has done exactly what God has told us not to do. Since mankind has never seen God, any image that they may create of Him will be a destortion and based, image-wise, on their own concept of what is most important to mankind themselves, or to the culture in which he or she resides. For example, the Israelites left Egypt with much wealth, especially GOLD for which to start a new life in the Promise Land, so it was gold that was important to them. And when they thought that Moses would not return from the mountain to continue leading them, they wanted another god to lead them, so what was the god that they created made from? you got it! Gold. That is because gold, as mention earlier, was the most important thing to them. Before I make my point however, allow me to make one thing perfectly clear, and that is, the biblical world was devoid of racism, and we can see this when we view the art works from ancient Egypt, Greece, and Rome; art works such as The Black

Pharaohs that conquered Egypt, Queen Kawit of Nubia, Queen Tiye, grandmother of King Tut, The Egyptian Princess who was the Queen of Sheba and was the wife of King Solomon, Zipporah, a descendent of Cush who was the wife of Moses and many, many more. Such art work shows a very clear awareness in art forms as such art forms related to the racial features and skin tones, however, there is little to no evidence that dark skin was ever seen as a sign of inferiority. As a matter of fact, Abraham's wife Sarah, actually talked him into having sex with Hagar, the dark skin Egyptian maidservant in order that she and Abraham could have the child that she thought she could not have, when that child was born they gave him the name of Ishmel. Now, had not God Intervened, the dark skin Hagar would have become the foremother of God's chosen people. On the other hand, when we observe the artwork of mankind in today's western world that depicts God, one can see that unlike in biblical times, color and race is very prominent, now why is that? Well, it is because in the western world color and race draws the line between those who have and those who have not, between those with power and those with limited power, between those who excel and those who are discouraged from excelling. So, since social and financial power in the western part of the world rests primarily among the Caucasian race of people, which is the way it was designed to be, God is therefore depicted as looking like a descendent of the Caucasian race, with their complexion and racial features, along with blue eyes and straight hair to boot. Now when one makes the comparison between the Israelites' choice of gold when they created their god, to today's western world's choice of changing God's color and features to that of the Caucasian race, one can see that there are paralles; you see the Israelites' sin was creating a god made from gold which is based on wealth, and the Western World depictions of God and even His Son is based on color, which in itself represents another form of wealth and privilege in the western world. In any event, it is a sin to create or distort the image of God or His Son. If however this is something that these artists in the western world just had to do, then their research should come from the bible and not from their minds. Allow me to explain, you see in the bible in the book of Revelation 1:12–15, John the Baptist give us a description of his Heavenly vision of Jesus Christ and he describes Jesus as one with snow white WOOLY hair with a BRONZE skin tone. Well now, this is a long way from the Caucasian looks that many artists in the western world have given to both God and his Son Jesus Christ. When one knows better it would appear that the western world is trying to justify the absence of deity of color in the Bible. To fully measure the full impact of such distortions, allow me to share with you some of my personal observations over the years when I visited many African Americans households; as I entered, there was always three pictures prominently placed on a given wall for all who entered to see, and who were those pictures of? Well one was of Jesus Christ, one was of John F. Kennedy and one was of Martin Luther King Jr., now guess which one was, and still is, distorted, you got it, Jesus Christ! You see when the spiritual legends rather than the spiritual fact are continually perpetuated, then the real lack of theological knowledge is experienced by all of us, both blacks and whites. Let's explore other distorted legends of people in the Bible. The actor Jim Caviezel that starred in The Passion of The Christ, did look like the created legend, but did not look like Jesus Christ. Charlton Heston who starred as Moses and Yvonne De Carlo who starred as his wife in the movie The Ten Commandments, did not look like Moses or his wife Zepporah, however they did look like the created legends. Although Cecil B. Demille and Mel Gibson did an excellent job of telling and directing their respective stories, they nevertheless did an inaccurate job Of casting in their respective movies, however I do realize that in the case of Cecil B. DeMills, during the time that he made his movie if he had utilized accurate biblical casting, then the movie itself could not have been made, due to the extent of racism that existed at that time in the late fifties. It is well known you see that only inferior, demeaning roles were reserved for people of color. This was not the case however when the movie The Passion of The Christ was made, you see much of the extreme racism that existed during the filming of the Ten Commandments had subsided. I am not surprised by such historical bias, because when one actually study most history closely, be it religious history or otherwise, one will find that in most cases it has been the created legends and not the facts as they existed that have been brought forth and expanded on, especially in the western world. To add further creditability to this view, just look at the people that are currently located in Africa and the Middle East, and what you will find even after thousands of years and much racial assimilation, the people that are located in these geographical areas are still people of a darker color, with facial features that are totally different from those of the Caucasian race. Even with this living proof, today's artists and authors' works still reflect a strong disregard for factual history. Or in other words, they still continue to perpetuate the created legends and not the facts as they existed or as they exist.

AN IGNORED CHAPTER OF HISTORY
TELLS OF A TIME WHEN KINGS FROM DEEP IN

AFRICA

CONQUERED ANCIENT

EGYPT

Black
Pharaohs

BY ROBERT DRAPER
NATIONAL GEOGRAPHIC CONTRIBUTING WRITER

PHOTOGRAPHS BY KENNETH GARRETT

Nubian pharaoh Taharaa (left) was buried in an Egyptian-style pyramid (above, left) in Sudan.

Statues of Nubian kings up to ten feet high were found buried at the Nubian capital of Kerma, in Sudan. Smashed during Egyptian King Psamtek II's incursion south around 593 B.C., they were recently reassembled.

Did the powerful Queen Tiye, King Tut's grandmother, have Nubian ancestry? This bust, made of wood that has darkened with age, has inspired claims that she did.

Nubia was a major source of gold for ancient Egypt. At Thebes the tomb of King Tutankhamun's viceroy to Nubia—a man named Huy—shows Nubian royalty in procession delivering rings of gold as part of their tribute to their overlord. The skilled goldsmiths of Nubia created masterpieces such as a pendant of the goddess Isis (right) from the tomb of a Nubian king at Nuri.

Queen Kuwit, shown on her sarcophagus having her hair dressed, was one of the noble women believed to have been sent from Nubia to make diplomatic marriages with 11th-dynasty pharaoh Mentuhotep II.

| Share

Map: Africa

Africa Profile: History · Government · Economy · Population ...

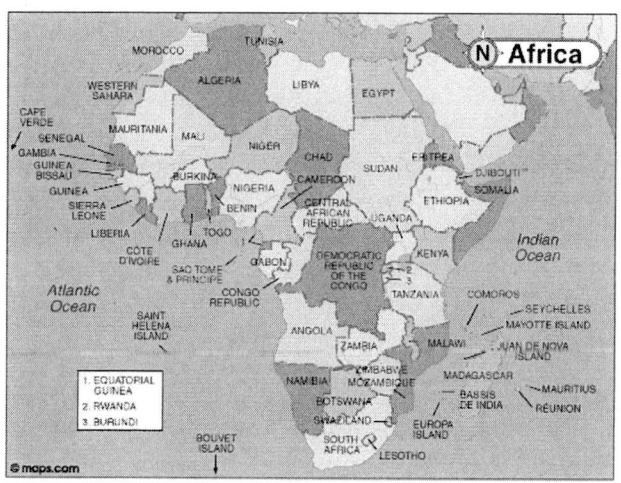

Africa Information

Encyclopedia: Africa

In-depth entries covering: Economy, Government, History, Land & People

More on Africa: Oceans and Continents

World Atlas · Map Index

Maps — Africa

Countries

Algeria	Libya
Angola	Madagascar
Benin	Malawi
Botswana	Mali
Burkina Faso	Mauritania
Burundi	Mauritius
Cameroon	Morocco
Cape Verde	Mozambique
Central African Republic	Namibia
Chad	Niger

Related Content

- Distance Calculator
- Latitude/Logitude Search
- Current Events
- Highest Mountains
- Oceans & Seas
- Largest Islands
- World Capitals
- Languages by Countries

| Share

Map: Middle East

Middle East Profile: History · Government · Economy · Population ...

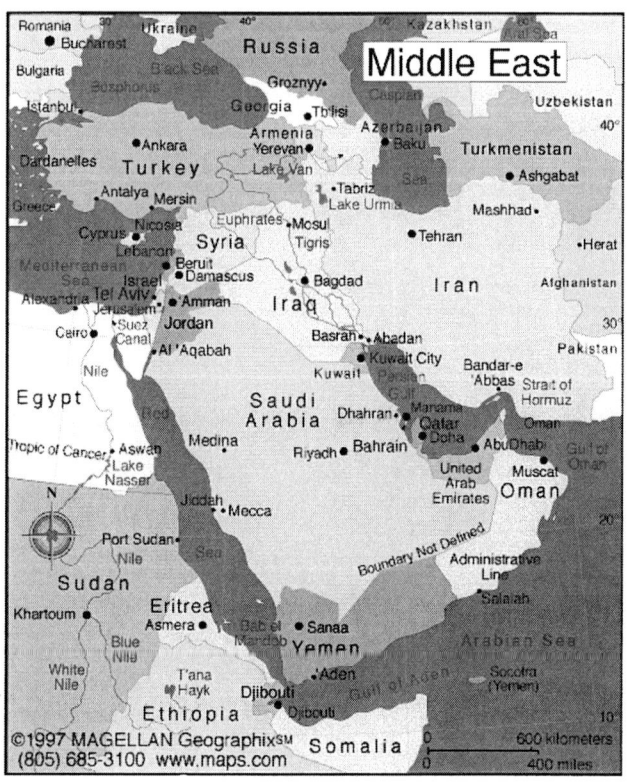

Middle East Information

Encyclopedia: Middle East

http://www.infoplease.com/atlas/middleeast.html   1/21/2011

Note: The Middle East is a loosely defined geographic region. Most of the Middle East countries are part of the Asia, with the exception of Egypt, which is part of Africa, and the northwestern part of Turkey, which is part of the European landmass.

What we should always keep in our minds is that almighty God created each and every one of us in his own image, and if we really wanted to see how God looks, then we should be willing to wait until he manifest his image in us. Remember Jesus' meeting with the Samaritan woman at the well and he told her that she should worship God in spirit and in truth, well that advice sounds to me like we should worship what we cannot see (since we cannot see our souls/spirits) and, we should do it truthfully, which calls into focus our faith. When God, through his Son, Jesus Christ does resurrect us from our long deathly sleep and the dust of our bodies return to the dust from which we were made, then, and only then, will our souls reflect the image of God, because that is when God will appear in full view for all to see. But until that time comes, the message given to us in the Bible is perfectly clear, and that is, all other renditions of God's image are creatively distorted and they are sinful; it was a sin when the Israelites created their idol god made from gold and changing God's color and facial features still remains a sin today, although mankind continues to do it. So, the next time you go to church, look at all of the beautiful stained glass windows and large crucifixes that are constructed with Caucasian images of Christ for all to see, and when you do, think about God' commandment about creating/ distorting the image of God; then you should ask yourself, WHO ARE THE PHARISEES AMONG US? On the other hand, I feel that all is not lost, because I've had an opportunity to view some of the works of some of today's authors and artists and I see authentic works coming forth, works like Schindler's List, Something The Lord Made, Hotel Rwanda, The Great Debaters (filmed at Wiley College my Alma Mater), The Blind Side and the two book written by then Senator Barack H. Obama entitled, Dreams From My Father and The Audacity of Hope; also in this category is, Can You See What I See (written by yours truly).

It is these types of works that portray God's people with both their true struggles along with their true accomplishments. It is when works like the above penetrate our worldly societies that our cultural knowledge is awaken. A WISE MAN ONCE SAID THAT HISTORY IS NOT ALWAYS WHAT IS WRITTEN, HOWEVER, HISTORY IS ALWAYS WHAT HAS HAPPENED! What is unique about the above books and movies is that they are based on true events that took place in our life time, but in all these stories there appears to have been a Moses like character that was placed by God and given the accountability in some shape or form, to deliver God's people from some form of suffering or social abuse. So you see, we don't have to guess or speculate about God working in our lives through others, all we have to do is to evaluate the factual history of those people living among us today, and not be guided by the distorted created history. When this is done, we will then have an opportunity to expose ourselves to how God's mighty works influence and guide our lives.

If we are true Christians, then we should know that when the lives of people, or a nation of people are creatively distorted, it is not only the lives of those people, or that nation that have been distorted, but such creative distortions deprives us of the vision to truly see God's plan and will for those people or nations. You see, God loves for us to have life and have life more abundantly. We witness this when we view the Israelites struggles, moving from four hundred years of slavery and then moving from a period of attempted social extermination to where they are today, running their own country, a country that was promised to them by God and delivered to them. We can also see it in the struggling history of the Africans who were brought to the western world, sold into slavery, bred like farm animals in order to increase the wealth of their slave owners, beaten and mutilated whenever they attempted to escape and above all they were kept educationally ignorant in hopes of voiding any quality of life in the future. Then, after some two hundred plus years, we have been blessed with the vision to witness these same slaves' descendants' long and difficult journey to recovery, a recovery that has taken them from being known and treated as the most inferior human beings of the face of this earth, to achieving the successful election of America's first African American President, Mr. Barack H. Obama by a majority vote, while still, mind you, being the minority population!! Now, as with Moses, Mr. Obama's steps were directed long before he went into politics believe me. You see, God loves to reflect his power With a strong hand as Moses stated in his conversation with God. Moses' statement has been proven true over and over again here on this earth and the impact can be measured both in the life struggles and accomplishments of those among us who have been enslaved and oppressed by others; what we have witnessed is God's plan being worked against mankind's sinful will. It is for this reason that we, as Americans should feel extremely blessed about the way God has so far, preserved and protected our great country. However, we as Christians must first of all recognize that it is God's will that continue to prevail and not ours. So now maybe we can see why distorting history in any form is, in itself sinful, because it deprives us of the visual knowledge of God's plan and will for our lives. Remember, without God we cannot and without us God won't. On the other hand, we should ask ourselves if those people among us who are creating the distortions in questions have an even more sinister reason for doing so, and could their reason be that the physical appearance of Jesus Christ when he walked this earth doesn't fit with western mankind's perceived deity of color superiority, as a result, it makes it very difficult for anyone holding such beliefs to follow and practice the teachings and living examples of a Jesus Christ with wool like hair and a bronze colored skin. Now if this is the case, then it is not only a sin, but such people that harbor such beliefs are already spiritually dead, they are just continuing to exist. Allow me to say at this point that while we are riding in this vehicle called history, we should acquire for ourselves a comfortable seat of faith, sit back, relax and open the window of our minds, and when we do, the incoming fresh air will clear the fog from our sights, thus allowing us to see the destination of where we are going by truly understanding exactly where we and others like us have been. My friends, our destination is God's Kingdom on earth having descended from heaven where there is absolutely no distortions! On the other hand, those people who have demonstrated a misguided spirituality with their hate filled physical activities directed toward a targeted group of God's people, well maybe, just maybe, they are giving us a realistic view of where they will spend their eternal salvation; remember, if they bring hell to earth, then hell is where they will spend their eternal lives, it's their choice. Now that I have made my point, I will return to the remaining commandment that is being given to Moses by God and they are: You shall not misuse the name of the Lord. Remember the Sabbath and keep it Holy. You should do all of your work in six days, but the seventh day is the Sabbath to your Lord God. Honor your father and your mother, so that they may live in the land that the Lord is giving you. You shall not kill. You shall not commit adultery. You shall not steal. You shall not give false testimony against your neighbor. You shall not covet your neighbor's wife, or his manservant or his maidservant, or his ox, or his donkey, or anything that belongs to your neighbor. Now, all during the time that God was speaking, the mountain was in smoke and the thunder roared, while lighting flickered.

Seeing this, the children of Israel trembled with fear. And while they made sure to stand at a good distance from the mountain, they pleaded to Moses saying: "Speak to us yourself Moses and we will listen. But don't have God speak to us for we will die." Moses responded to the people by saying: "Do not be afraid, God has come to test you so that the fear of God will be with you to keep you from sinning." So now our story continues to move along, and although we are still in the Old Testament, we are about to see the different accountabilities that God had for Abraham as opposed to Moses; you see with Abraham God's assigned accountabilities for him was his righteousness, his obedience and his ability to segment God's chosen people from others and then keep them together. However with Moses, God had made him accountable for leading them out of four hundred years of bondage, then giving them laws and decrees to live by and then lead them into an orderly society in the land that he had promised to Abraham. The Bible you see represents God's one plan, but with two strategies in which different accountabilities were assigned to different people. And in order to accomplish God's plan, each person that was made accountable by God, utilized their respective God given talents in order to accomplish God's goals. When we move into the New Testament, we will witness new people with new accountabilities as well, and the goals for which they will be held accountable will be based on their God given talents to achieve such goals, this includes Jesus Christ as well. Now, because these different strategies and accountabilities were prevalent, it should not mean that we should believe and practice one part of the Bible and not the other part, because as I stated earlier, the Bible is one plan by God with two parts that includes assigned strategies which were set forth to accomplish God's one overall objective, and that is the Eternal Salvation for all mankind. Since God's plan is still continuing on today, then we should understand that the accountabilities that were assigned during biblical times are still being assigned today, the question is however, are we aware of what God is holding us accountable for?

In any event, as we continue our story, God is giving his Ten Commandments to Moses which is intended for controlling mankind's behavior toward God and mankind's society. You see mankind cannot have an orderly society unless mankind's behavior toward others is equally as orderly. As I alluded to earlier, God's communications when he spoke were extremely specific, and even though the laws and decrees were many, if my memory serves me correctly over six hundred, nevertheless they were still specific, for example, there were laws on how to build a Tabernacle, laws on what garments the Priests should wear, even laws on how such garments should be made, laws about hygene were given, as well as what to eat, ect.... God's efforts to change the Israelites' behavior from that of being slaves to that of Priests representing a Holy Nation took time, patience, planning and yes, laws, laws in which every single one that was instituted was needed. It was at this time in my researching for this book, that God blessed me to understand and to see His glorious plan, and for that I am greatful. Lets return to the story where we find Moses once again has return to the mountain top because God is now ready to put His Ten Commandments in written form. When Moses arrived at the top of the mountain, God told him to carve out two stone tablets and He would write His Commandments on them and Moses obeyed. All in all, Moses was with God some forty days and forty nights, during which time he was allowed to look only upon God's back but not his face; for to have looked upon God's face would have ment death for Moses. Because Moses was gone too long, the Israelites' slave mentality dictated that they needed a leader that would lead them in Moses' absence. So they gathered around Aaron, the brother of Moses, and said to him "come, make us a god that will go before us as Moses did when he brought us out of Egypt, because we don't know what has happened to him. Aaron, who at the time was a Priest of the people, relented and to complete their wish, he accepted the most powerful and important thing that they had, and that was their gold. Aaron melted the gold down, then he shaped it into the form of a calf and in doing this Aaron and the Israelites had done exactly what God had commanded them not to do and that was to create a idol god. And, on top of this sin, the israelites furthered their sinful ways by committing adulterous acts. Knowing just what had happened, when the Lord completed writing the Ten Commandments on the two tablets of stone, He spoke to Moses in a very angry voice saying, "go down, because the people that you brought out of Egypt, have become corrupt. They have been quick to turn away from what I commanded of them and they have made themselves an idol cast in the shape of a calf. They have bowed down to it and they have sacrificed to it and they have said, "This is our god of Israel who brought us out of Egypt." God continued His angry venting by telling Moses, I have seen these people and they are stiff-neck people. Now leave me alone so that my anger may burn against them and that I may destroy them. Then, I will make you into a great nation." Now, it was at this point that I had second thoughts about every repetitive sin that I ever committed in my life, and I actually stop typing on my computer long enough to ask for God forgiveness, because it is here in the story that God shows us that not only does He have patience and much love for us, but at some point and time our sinful ways anger Him to the point that He wishes to destroy us. So I prayed to Jesus Christ our Lord and Savior to keep me from becoming a stiff-neck person; a person that is unwilling to turn from their sinful ways. Nevertheless, when Moses heard the anger of the Lord, he sought the favor of his God. And as Moses started to make his plea for forgiveness from God, we now see just how closely Moses had paid attention to God's proclamation to the Jewish people, because Moses started to remind God of His plan by saying: "Lord why should your anger burn against your people whom you brought out of Egypt with a great power and a mighty hand? Don't allow the Egyptians to say that it was with evil intent that He brought them out to kill them in the mountians and to wipe them off the face of the earth. Turn from your fierce anger, relent, do not bring disaster on your own people. Remember your servants, Abraham, Isaac and Jacob to whom you swore by your own self: I will make your descendents as numerous as the stars in the sky and I will give your descendents all of the land that I promised them, and it will be their land forever." After hearing Moses, God relented and did not bring on His people the disaster that He had threatened. After Moses had made his prayerful request to God and God had relented, Moses then turn and again went down the mountain. The two tablets that he held in his arms were the work of God, the writing was the writing of God, and when Moses met Joshua at the foot of the mountain, they both were able to hear loud noises of people shouting. Joshua said to Moses, "there is a sound of war in the camp." And Moses replied, "It is not the sound of defeat and it is not the sound of victory, it is the sound of singing that I hear." As Moses approched the camp, he saw the people dancing around the golden calf, Moses anger burned and he lifted the two tablets of stone over his head and then threw them down where they landed at the foot on the mountain, breaking them into many pieces. He then took the calf that Aaron had sculptured and burned it in the fire, ground it into power, scattered it on the water and made the Israelites drink it. Moses then turned to his brother Aaron who he had left in charge saying: "What did these people do to you that you led them into such a great sin?" Do not be angry my lord answered Aaron, for you know how prone these people are to evil. They said to me: Make us a god that will go before us, because this fellow Moses who brought us out of Egypt, well we don't know what has happened to him." So I told them to give me their jewelry, when they did, I threw them into the fire and out came this calf (as if by divine order). Now it was this sin and subsequent divine lie by Aaron that would change his destination from the Promise Land to his final resting place of Mount Hor, where he died because he did not uphold God's Holiness among the Israelites and he broke faith with God. In the meantime Moses saw that the people were running wild because Aaron had allowed them to get out of control. But we are about to see that same sense of justice from Moses that caused him to save the slave woman life in Egypt start to emerge, when he stood at the entrance of the camp and shouted to the people: "Whoever is for the Lord come to me" and all of the Levites came to him. Moses then told the Levites to take up their swords and go back through the camp killing brothers, friends and neighbors. They did as Moses commanded and at the end of the day, some three thousand people from the Twelve Tribes of Israel had been executed. When it was all over, Moses went back up the mountain to seek forgiveness from God for his people, saying: Oh what a great sin these people have committed! They have made themselves a god of gold. But now please forgive their sin, however, if you do not, then take me out of the book of life that you have written. It is here in this very conversation with God that Moses truly demonstrated a love that the Greeks calls the AGAPE LOVE (love of the soul of others leading to care for their welfare), yes this is the love that Moses had for the Israelites. Now when we read the New Testament, we will find in the chapter of John 21:15–17, Jesus asked Peter three times if he loved him and each time Peter's answer demonstrated a different love that the Greeks call PHILEO LOVE (a brotherly type love for someone). You see Peter, just like many of us today, we find that our love for God is not inclusive; for God wants us not only to love Him but to love his people as well and to take care of their well being. So if we are to love God in the manner that he wants us to love him, then we must include in our love of God the love of the souls that he created as well. Moses had this type of love and he demonstrated it in his plea to God. However, at the time that God asked Peter, such love was not a part of Peter's love for Christ, although he would eventually acquire such love when the Holy Spirit descended upon him. Continuing, in this meeting with God, Moses received an answer from God when God said: "Whoever sinned against me I will blot out of my book." Today as I witness how the poor, sick and homeless people of God's creation are treated and negatively talked about by the so called Christians in our present society, I am stunned because what they call socialism, I call love, AGAPE LOVE! I also wonder if they realize that God is telling them each and every day that they cannot love him unless they both love and be willing to care for those needy souls that he has created. Also another rule of God is: It is not enough to be knowledgeable about the scriptures in the Bible, but we are also compelled to live out the meaning of those scriptures in our everyday lives.

Our story continues when God tells Moses to go ahead and lead the people to the land that he spoke of, he also told Moses that he would send an Angel to go before him, and when the time came he would punish them for their sin. And so it was, the Lord placed a plague on the people for what they had done with the gold calf that Aaron had made. Then the Lord told Moses to take the people that he had led out of Egypt and leave the place where they were camped and to go to the land that he had promised to Abraham, Isaac and Jacob, saying: "I will give it to your descendents." God then dispatched an Angel before them to drive out the Amorites, the Hittites, the Perizzites, the Hivites and the Jebusites. Go, God said, up to the land flowing with milk and honey. But I will not go with you even for a moment, for I might destroy you. Here we see that God's patience with the Israelites did grow extremely thin, but Moses, being the faithful servant that he was, acted as an effective intermediator and it was because of Moses' love for God and God's people (the AGAPE LOVE), that the journey to the Promise Land remained on course.

As the Twelve Tribes of Israel remained on their journey, their numbers had been reduced by some three thousand fellow tribesmen, and those that were not killed when Moses gave the orders, were struck with the plague that God sent. So as we continue to follow this story which is taking place in the Old Testament, we see that when God was accountable for the direct interaction with mankind as he was with Moses and the Israelites, Initially there were no laws and because of the lack of laws, Moses had to rule the Israelites with the laws and decrees that were given to him by God. Also, there were consequences for not obeying the laws and decrees that were set forth by God. Nevertheless, a time was coming with the introduction of the New Testament when God would implement a new world order, after which, God will relinquish his accountability to his Son, Jesus Christ. When this transition takes place mankind's eternal salvation will be based on two things: His faith and his acceptance that Jesus Christ is the Son of God. If mankind makes the wrong decision, and he has the free will to do so, then and only then will God's justice prevail through his Son Jesus Christ on the day of judgment. This is the difference between The Old and New Testaments and why the Bible has separated us by the way that we worship, our religion. As we return to our story, Moses has been called back to visit with God, Moses has been instructed by God to chisel out two more stones like the ones that he had broken. When Moses finished chiseling the two stones, God rewrote the Ten Commandments and when Moses descended back down the mountain, his face was glowing with the glory of the Lord even though his meeting with God had not been face to face. The writing on the two stone tablets that Moses carried in his arms still, to this day, govern our moral and spiritual lives because the Ten Commandments, via the Jewish nation has been preserved throughout our world history. Continuing however, we see that God makes a change in his assigned accountability from Moses to Joshua, and Moses tells Joshua the warrior that he would be the one that will lead the people of Israel to the Promise Land. Shortly after this historical transition, and on what was truly a sad day in the history of the Israelites, Moses' death finally came on Mount Nebo, in the plains of Moab. But before Moses died, God did show him the Promise Land and reminded Moses that he would give it to the descendents of Abraham, Isaac and Jacob. But God told Moses that he would not be allowed to enter because of his sin when he entered the land in Rephidim (that is when Moses angrily lashed out at God because of the complaining Israelites and it was pointed out that Moses trip to the Promise Land had ended, but not his journey). History tells us that Moses died in Moab, the valley opposite Beth Peor, however, to this day no one has been able to locate the grave; it is for this reason that many believe that God allowed his most loyal and faithful servant to assend to heaven to be with him. History also tells us that there will never be another Prophet or Prophets with the powerful hand of the Prophet Moses.

Now that we have been able to see how God the Father interacted directly with and through mankind in the Old Testament by tracing God's involvement through Abraham, Isaac and Jacob, on through the Prophets and through Moses, who he assigned the responsibility of leading his people out of Egypt, and implementing the Ten Commandments, plus giving him other laws and decrees, and above all, God held Moses responsible for training and informing the Israelites when their conduct conflicted with God's laws. But now we see the accountabilities of God's plan being transferred over to Joshua; and it would be Joshua and not Moses, who would lead the Children of Israel into the land of milk and honey. So when the walls of Jericho fell because of the leadership of Joshua, but not without God's will, the Children of Israel did occupy their new land. But now they would become the ones who have, instead of the ones who have not. So, how would they deal with the have not in their new land. Well, their instructions from God was loud and clear. When we examine Leviticus 25:14–17 and 35–38, we see that Moses had already given God's specific guidelines to the Israelites as to how their neighbors/countrymen, that had less should be treated when business is conducted with them. These eight verses were not only applicable for the Israelites and their new society, but, when one reads them, one will see that the honesty and lack of greed are just as applicable to the banks and other loan institutions in our societies today. In any event, what is perfectly clear throughout these verses is the warning from God that if his rules are not followed, then the ones breaking the rules should fear him. Now when we see our neighbors today loosing their homes to foreclosures due to unfair loan practices, or the inability to acquire a home loans, or tricked into signing loans contracts that they could not afford, should we not ask ourselves, WHO ARE THE PHRISEES AMONG US?

In part two of this book, The Pharisees will now have the accountability for managing not only the Roman laws, but also managing the Ten Commandments that were handed down from Moses, as well as the many other laws and decrees affecting the Children of Israel in their new land. It is in part two of this book that we will evaluate the methods by which the Pharisees, as contemporaries of Jesus Christ, executed this phase of God' plan. But before moving on, let me remind those of you who feel that because the Jewish people hearts had harden and they continually rejected and sinned against God, that God, in turn, turned from them. And as a result, their souls are lost and the salvation that was promised to them is also lost. Well, allow me to say that such feelings are not true. What is true however, is that when God chose the Jews as His race of people for His Son to be born into, the promise that He made to Abraham, Isaac and Jacob became totally irrovacable. Also, one must understand that had the Jews not rejected Jesus as the Son Of God, then the Gentiles, or those of us that are not Jewish, would have never been grafted onto God's tree of salvation; for it was the space that was made available on God's tree of salvation after the Jewish branches had fallen off, that made our inclusion possible. This process gave the Gentiles their opportunity for eternal salvation. Being grafted onto God's tree, means that the Gentiles are now allowed to share in the nourishing sap that flows from the roots of the olive tree (Romans 11:17–21). These two verses also tells us not to boast about being grafted onto God's tree; for if we do, we should consider this: It is not us that support the roots, but the roots that supports us. God also tells us not to be arrogant, but instead we should be afraid; for if God did not spare the natural branches, which represents the fallen Jews, then He will not spare the grafted on wild branches, which represents the Gentiles. So, when all is said and done, The Gentiles' salvation depends on the room that was made available on the tree, it is because of this that the Gentiles are now exposed to the word of God through His Son Jesus Christ. And it is through our faith and His mercy that we will be saved. Oh, by the way, this is the same mercy that He will extend to the Jews that have rejected His Son, Jesus Christ. Should we judge? under no circumstances should we judge the Jews or anyone else, because God has told us not to judge. However, understanding the message that the fallen Jews have sent, and in many cases, still sending, tells us that we should monitor our own lives and when we do, we too will then see just how difficult it is to stay focus on God's Son as our Lord and Savior and follow His living examples while He was here on this earth. Always remember, knowledge about the bible without living out the messages by God and His Son, Jesus Christ in the bible, is, and always will be, a non starter. Before moving on to part two of this book, I would like to give you an example, a real world example of how we loose our spiritual focus. When I was about sixteen years of age, and living in my hometown of Dallas, Texas, my family like so many other African Americans families at that time throughout the United States, had started to migrate from the central city areas to the suburbs. When we made the move, my family selected a large three bedroom upstairs suite located on South Boulevard Street. The downstairs suite was already occupied by a Jewish family. This Jewish family had one son by the name of Bernie.

Bernie was about twelve years of age and he truly loved baseball, and since I played the game and played it extremely well, Bernie deeply respected my God given talents. Every time Bernie could get me to play catch with him in our front yard, he would do so, and I inturn would take that time to coach him in the finer details of the game as best I could. One Friday when I returned home from my baseball practice at my high school, as I approched the front yard I saw Bernie playing catch with himself. Bernie had an old worn-out beseball glove that he adored. As I approched Bernie, I spoke and told him how excited I was that my school was buying me a new baseball glove and that the glove would have a deep web for trapping the baseball; I explained exactly how important this feature was to the position that I was playing, which was shortstop. Bernie stated that he was very happy for me, but, as he made that statement, I could see that his big brown eyes appeared to grow very sad as he looked down at his old glove that he had cherished for years. I could tell from Bernie's reactions that once he had heard my good news, the old glove that he had grown to love, instantly became bad news. Realizing what I was seeing, I placed my arm around Bernie's skinny shoulders in hopes of silently consoling him, and as we turned and walked toward our housing complex. It was at that time that I told Bernie that I would be going to Sears the next morning (which was on a Saturday) to purchase the new glove that my school, Saint Peters' Academy was buying for me. As we reached the front steps, we said goodbye to each other and I continued on to my family's upstairs suite. At around 8:30am that Saturday morning our doorbell rang and my mother who happened to be up at the time, answered the door by speaking through an in-wall greeting pipe that ran from our suite upstairs to an opening in the wall next to our front door downstairs. The voice that I heard talking back to my mother was that of Bernie's father. He ask my mother if he could speak with me. I promptly went downstairs to speak with him. As I arrived at the door and opened it, we greeted each other, while at the same time shaking hands. Bernie's father stated that he knew that I would be going to Sears for the purpose of purchasing a beseball glove, and he asked if I would be so kind to purchase a glove for his son Bernie just like the one that I would be getting? I responded by telling him that I would be more than happy to do just that and, if there was anything else that he wanted me to do? He said no, but, he quickly followed that short reply up by saying that he would do it himself but that it was the Sabbath day for his family, as such, they were not allowed to do any work or make any purchases. I then told Bernie's father that when I return from Sears, I would bring the glove to him. He thanked me and we parted ways. However, as I made my way back upstairs I was thinking to myself that if his religion actually band purchaces on the Sabbath, then it was still wrong for him to make any purchases through me, since it was him that initiated the purchases when he gave me the money. And, as I saw things, even with my sixteen year old mind at the time, it didn't matter to God that the glove was picked up by me, the sin according to the Jewish Religion as he had explained it to me that morning in 1953, was still committed by Bernie's father and not me. However, because of the love that this father had for his son, plus the need to make him happy, this otherwise loving Jewish father had sinned. Even today when I think about this incident by Bernie's father, which still remain imbedded in my mind, I see it as a perfect example of how we, as good God fearing people become caught up in worldly things, even the love of our families can cause us to stray away from our faithful convictions; and in the process, we end up placing God in the position of second place in our lives. This is exactly what the love of his son had made Bernie's father do. When we move on to part two of this book, we will find that the Pharisees were a lot like Bernie's father, they were well meaning if their efforts to interpret and manage God's laws and decrees, but because they were men that were influenced by the world, they had a tendency to allow the worldly temptations to consume them and in doing so, they became very good at implementing and enforcing God's laws but, at the same time, they themselves did not follow such laws. For instance, the animals that they used for sacrificies on the Alter were unhealthy, deformed animals and they set aside the healthy animals for their financial gain. Because of their actions, the sacrifices that they offered up to God were rejected because of their hypocrisy and transgressions. As I continued to research the background of the Pharisees, my rsearch made me reflect back on a Pharisacal moment that I had the Easter before writing this book; you see our oldest son had been transferred by his job from Philidelphia, Pa. to Tulsa, Ok., which was only 4 hours from our home in Plano, Tx...This was a move that both my wife and I had prayed for. In any event, our son and his wife, along with our two grandsons had driven down to visit with us for Easter. Also joining us was our youuungest son and his wife along with our only grand daughter. For this occasion, my wife and I had prepared a big Texas size dinner, consisting of a large smoked ham, bar-be-que ribs with all of the trimmings. Early that Easter Sunday morning we all got dressed and made our way to church services. When we returned from church, we had arranged for our dinner to be sevred buffet style, which ment that everyone would serve themselves. For the grand children my wife had purchased gifts for Easter consisting of toy bonnie rabbits, ducks and large plastic eggs. When the toy eggs were twisted open, the surprise that was found inside, were little toy cars. After everyone had finish eating, we gave out the gifts, and as the children were playing with their gifts, my youngest grandson, Hunter, who was seven years of age at that time, ask me a very penetrating question, he said: "Grand Pâ Pâ, what do all of these ducks, cars and bonnie rabbits have to do with Easter? As I turn in complete amazement and looked at him, I starred into his big brown eyes, and while facing the full impact of his question, I searched for an answer. Then I realized that an explanation about the toys was not the answer that he was expecting, so I impetuously answered by saying: Hunter, absolutely nothing! Then I followed up by telling him the story of Jesus' death and resurrection. You see, in the process of sharing our love with our family by preparing a meal that reflected that love along with the gifts that we had given, still we had nothing in our presentation that said anything about Jesus, His death or His resurrection. As a matter of fact, I don't recall that we even blessed the meal. I know now in retrospect that we had prepared ourselves to celebrate Easter alright, but in our actions my wife and I had actually forgot to include Jesus Christ. Instead, we had replaced our love for Jesus with the love and attention of our family. My grandson's question allowed me to recognize that our efforts were spiritually remiss, and as the patriarch of my family, I had done a very poor job of keeping my family's focus on the true meaning of Easter.

Now as far as my grandson's question, well, I guess that was God's way of reminding me through my grandson's question that he always expect for his Son to be first in our lives. Easter you see, is not about the love of our families or anything else on this earth, it is however about Jesus Christ's love for us and his victory over death which assures our resurrection. So, as you read about the Pharisees and their actions and relationship with Jesus Christ in part two of this book, one should be extremely careful not to judge them, but, one should take what they learn from them and in doing so, examine your own lives as I have mine. When this is done, hopefully we will be able to proactively adjust our spiritual lives so that Jesus Christ, our Lord and Savior will always be front and center in this world as it is today. If we are unable to do this, then we should ask ourselves this important question; WHO ARE THE PHAR- ISEES AMONY US?

PART TWO

THE NEW TESTAMENT
THE NEW LIGHT THAT COMETH
INTO THE WORLD

As with any people or group of people, in order to fully understand and appreciate their times in history, one must have some understanding not just of their accomplishments as to what they expected of themselves during their historical time period but in the study of such people, one must ask oneself, did they accomplish their expectations? Well, when we observe the Pharisees, we will see that they were very well educated, certainly much more educated than the rest of the Jewish society that they had the responsibility of governing. In addition, they were very well versed about all of God's Commandments that were handed down from Moses himself and they were also aware of all of the Roman laws; as such, they occupied positions of power on the Council that sat in judgment of the people, making sure that the Commandments as well as the Decrees were strictly adhered to. And, when the laws and decrees were broken, then it was the Pharisees that made sure the respective law breakers were punished utilizing either the Jewish laws and decrees or the Roman laws to prove their guilt. The Pharisees also served as teachers within the society. The Temple they used for worship took some forty years to build and the homes that they lived in were conveniently connected to the Temple. Inside of their homes they had their very own bathing pools, so the Pharisees did not have to use the public bathing pools with the rest of the Jewish society. This life style put the Pharisees in the position of avoiding the very same people that they were responsible for ministering to, as well as teaching and leading by example. Now, it was this opulent life style, this indirect power and self imposed segregation and lustful greed that so conflicted with the way that Jesus Christ would live his life publicly, which would be among the poor, among the sick and among needy citizens other than Jewish citizens.

So, now we see that the Pharisees, who were expected to be leaders and Priest of a Holy Nation, were not fulfilling the expectations that were placed upon them; they were self removed from the very people that they were supposed to be closely leading spiritually. In the process of this spiritual abandonment, they had, in turn, lost all spiritual creditability with God and it was this spiritual synapse that had in turn pushed many of the Jewish people away from God's laws and decrees. Nevertheless, the Pharisees themselves practice distorted versions of these same laws and decrees for their own advantage. As a result of the hypocrisy of the Pharisees, more and more of the Jewish people were turning away from following such laws. And. The Temple that had taken some forty years to build, was being utilized for reasons other than worship, for example money was being exchanged, animals and expensive garments were being sold, ect,...It was these types of actions by the Jewish leaders of God's chosen people that would so drastically go against the teachings of God's only Son, Jesus Christ during the thirty three years that He would walk this earth. It would be these same thirty three years as we follow the Life of Jesus Christ in this story, that would set into motion the dramatic rise of Christianity as we know it today!

As we enter into the second part of our story, we find that Jesus has turned thirty years of age and already He has preached in the Temple at age twelve and

He has become a master carpenter. But now Jesus realizes that He must be about His Father's work and that work must start with His baptism by water, then He can get on with the job of baptizing His followers with the Holy Spirit. So, we find that Jesus is making His way down to Bethany which is on the other side of the Jordan River, there He will meet John The Baptist for His baptism. You see John the Baptist was sent by God to both witness and testify about the new light, that was coming into the world, so that through Him all men might believe. As John was baptizing, two very large crowd gathered; also the Jewish leadership had dispatched Priests and Levites to investigate. During their investigation, they were asking John all types of questions, Like: Are you the Christ? John answered: "I am not the Christ. Are you Elijah? John answered: "I am not." Are you the Prophet? John answered: "No." Finally they said who are you? Give us an answer that we can take back to those that sent us. John then replied, "I am the voice of one calling in the desert, make straight the way for the Lord." The next day while baptizing, John saw Jesus coming toward him and he said, "Look, the Lamb of God that takes away the sins of the world." Then John gave his testimony, saying, "I saw the Spirit come down from Heaven as a dove and remain on Him, I would not have known Him, except the one that sent me to baptize with water told me that the man on whom you see the Spirit come down and remain is he who will baptize with the Holy Spirit. I have seen and I testify that this is the Son of God." With this testimony by John the Baptist, Jesus is then baptized and when He emerged and walked from the river's water, at that same moment the world was also emerging and would never again be the same. The next day Jesus returned to the River Jordan where John was again baptizing, and again, the river was crowded with onlookers and people were waiting to be baptized. As Jesus worked His way through the massive crowd, John saw Him and cried out as He was passing, "Look, the Lamb of God." When two of John's disciples heard what he had said, they started to follow Jesus and they went to where He was staying and they stayed with him for around ten hours. Andrew, Simon Peter's brother was one of the disciples that stayed with Jesus and afterward the first thing that he did was to find his brother, Simon and he told him that they had found the Messiah and he then brought his brother to Jesus. Jesus looked at him and said, "You are Simon, son of John. You will be called Cephas (meaning Peter)." The next day Jesus moved on to Galilee, there He found Philip and said to him, follow me. Phillip did follow Jesus, and in the process, Phillip found Nathanael and told him about the Prophet that Moses had written about in the Law. And, so it was, God's plan through Jesus Christ was starting to take place and He would continue attracting the disciples that He would teach and train through example, so that long after He is gone they will be able to carry on with the new theology that He would bring to the world. Now even though Jesus had seven distressful reasons for meeting with the Pharisees in order to set them straight, for now that could wait because His first priority was to bring His message to the poor and teach and in doing so, He would be able to convert both the people and his disciples to the words of

God. But for now there was an important wedding that was to take place on the hills of Cana in Galilee. Nevertheless, the wedding that was to take place was not wanted by either the bridegroom or the bride; for it was to be the wedding of John The Baptist to Mary Magdalene. Now, the bible makes no mention of who would be married, only that a wedding took place. Maybe the reason the bible does not mention who is to be married is because the Jewish society as well as biblical history have been very successful in discrediting Mary Magdalene as a prostitute, of course such charges has been proven untrue and rescinded by the Magisterium of the Roman Catholic Church in 1969 nevertheless, because of this slanderous epithet, Mary Magdalene has never assumed her rightful place in the Church or in the biblical history that followed. This is another reason for so much of the gender bias in the bible. But if the bridegroom or the bride did not want to get married, then why was this marriage to take place? Good question! You see John the Baptist had many, many followers and many of them thought that He was the Messiah instead of Jesus. Also, The Pharisees were more in line with the strong, strict Jewish laws and religion advocated and preached by John the Baptist, plus the Jewish culture at the time demanded that for a man's life to be successful and complete, then he must be married with descendents, most specifically male descendents who would inherit the family's legacy. It is for this very same reason that many biblical scholars believe that Jesus Christ was married as well. Maybe one day someone will find yet another gospel hidden in the hot desert sands of Egypt like The Gospel of Mary Magdalene that was found buried in Egypt in 1945, and it will answer this very same question, was Jesus the Christ married? My dear friends, that would be a book worth writing about!! So, it is for this reason that I will continue my long pursuit in this area. However, returning to our story, we find that with the help of The Pharisees and the High Priest, Jonathan Annas, the wedding of John the Baptist to Mary Magdalene was on!

The reason that Mary, the mother of Jesus were attending the wedding along with Jesus and his disciples was because Jesus' mother, Mary was the first cousin to Elisabeth, who was the mother of John the Baptist, and since John's parents had died some time earlier, Mary knew that organizing a wedding was not one of John the Baptist strong points. True enough, when Jesus and his mother arrived, Mary determined that the wedding was running out of wine and she saw this as an opportunity to exalt her Son by exposing the hundreds of people present to God's only Son's ability to make a miracle. When Mary approached Jesus and requested his help to make more wine, Jesus stated that his time had not yet come and this was not his wedding. Mary then informed Jesus why she was asking because the wine was about gone and, she wanted to salvage the reputation of her cousin Elisabeth's family. So because of Mary's

ARTICAL TAKEN FROM THE DALLAS MORNING NEWS

THE WORLD'S OLDEST BIBLE
THE CODEX SINAITICUS

~~~~~~~~~~~~~~~~~~~~~~~

For oldest Bible, a divine new look

Once texts are digitally reunited, public can see and interpret changes

By TOD ROBBERSON
Europe Bureau

LONDON — Is the Bible the infallible word of God or a text doctored by calligraphers, priests and politicians to satisfy their own earthly motivations?

Evidence suggesting the latter is contained on the pages of the world's oldest Bible, the Codex Sinaiticus. The ancient Greek Bible, written between the first and fourth centuries, has been di-vided since the mid-1800s after visitors from Russia and Western Europe removed sections of it from a desert monastery in Egypt.

But on Thursday, experts from Britain, Germany, Russia, Egypt and the United States launched a four-year project to digitally re-unite the fragile texts and make them available to anyone with the click of a mouse.

"The codex is so special as a foundation document and a unique icon to Christianity," said John Tuck, head of British Collections at the British Library in London. Unification of the manu-

See **ANCIENT** *Page 20A*

Ancient Bible to go digital

Continued from Page 1A

script, even digitally, "is a block-buster in scholarship."

Only a privileged few have ever been allowed to handle the original manuscripts. Scholars need access to determine, among other things, how far the modern Bible has veered in interpretation from the codex. Parts of the project announced Thursday will include Christian texts written as few as 45 years after the death of Jesus Christ.

The manuscripts are so delicate that only four scholars have been granted access in the last 19 years to sections of the text housed in London, said Scot McKendrick, head of medieval and earlier manuscripts at the British Library in London.

But researchers and the general public will be able to examine the digitized texts in minute detail. Historical and explanatory notations will accompany the digitized texts so that viewers can trace how changes were made and, more important, why.

"Obviously, the way the editing works ... is exceedingly interesting. What is the process leading to this or that correction? Whether it was merely editorial, or if they were following a theological lead" in altering the message, Mr. McKendrick said.

Altered book

Ray Bruce, a film director who is producing a documentary on the project, cited the Book of Mark as an example of how much the modern Bible has been altered from the codex. In the codex, he said, the Book of Mark ends at Chapter 16, Verse 8, with the discovery that Christ's tomb was empty.

But more modern versions contain an additional 12 verses with testimony from Mary Magdalene and 11 apostles referring to the resurrection of Jesus.

"It shows how much this is a dynamic process of editing and

British Library

Biblical experts announced Thursday a four-year project at the British Library in London to digitally reunite the fragile texts of the world's oldest Bible.

ON THE WEB

Visit the British Library, the national library of the United Kingdom, at **www.bl.uk**

es questions about the influence man has had on texts regarded by Christians as divinely inspired.

Researchers and plunderers have particularly coveted the codex because the texts were written so soon after the life of Jesus, and they are the largest and longest-surviving biblical manuscript in existence, including both the Old and New Testaments. In addition, the codex contains two Christian texts written around A.D. 65, the Shepherd of Hermas and the Epistle of Barnabas.

Sections removed

Until the mid-1800s, the complete codex was housed inside St. Catherine's Monastery in Sinai, Egypt. But the texts were broken up when visitors bribed, cajoled or deceived monks into letting certain sections be removed for further examination in Russia, Britain and Germany.

"They were never returned," said Greek Orthodox Archbishop Damianos of Sinai. "The monastery felt a great injustice was done."

He said the disappearance of

the texts led to upheaval in the monastery, and because of lingering resentment, the monks at St. Catherine's had been "a bit reluctant to respond positively" when asked to participate in the current project.

In particular, he singled out Britain for criticism because of what he described as the underhanded manner in which it obtained its texts and its longtime refusal to return them. Nevertheless, he said, the monastery agreed to join the digitization project.

Other parts of the manuscript that had been taken to Russia disappeared after the 1918 Bolshevik Revolution and were feared lost forever. They did not reappear until the mid-1940s and are now kept at the National Library of Russia in St. Petersburg.

Going high-tech

Mr. McKendrick said the codex was originally produced on high-grade papyrus with state-of-the-art ink and pens — the best available at the time.

Similarly, the new digitization project will use some of today's most advanced technology, he added. "So in a sense, we'll be matching fourth century cutting edge technology with cutting edge 21st century technology."

E-mail trobberson@dallasnews.com

request Jesus turned the water to wine and when Jesus had finished, he asked the servant to take a cup to Caiaphas who was officiating the wedding ceremony. Caiaphas when he received the sample cup he tasted it, after which he lifted his cup to John the Baptist telling him that most people serve their best wine first and save the poor wine for last, but you have save the best wine for last. John looked at Caiaphas in total confusion, because neither he or the Priest had any knowledge of what had taken place. But, thanks to Mary it would not be long before everyone in Galilee would know exactly what had taken place at the wedding in Cana. After the wedding, Jesus along with his mother and disciples continued on to Jerusalem where he would visit the Temple; it would be this visit which would prove so provoking to those in power, the Pharisees, and set into motion Jesus' long, bloody, ruthless, but soul saving trip to that hill on Calvary. Nevertheless, when Jesus arrived at the Temple he entered through the Court Yard and there he found men selling sheep, cattle and doves, while others sat at tables exchanging money. Jesus, seeing all of this became extremely angry and he made a whip out of some cords and began whipping them out of the Temple area, including the sheep and cattle; he scattered the coins of the money changers and overturned the tables that they were using. And, to those that were selling doves, he said, "Get them out of here! I dare you turn my Father's house into a market." The Jews then demanded that Jesus show some type of miraculous sign that would prove His authority to do what he had done. So, speaking to what would be his final outcome, Jesus answered them saying, "Destroy this Temple and I will raise it again in three days." The Jews then replied, "It has taken some forty six years to build this Temple and you are going to raise it again in three days?" Of course the Jews were talking about the building itself, but Jesus was speaking about his body. Still, while Jesus was in Jerusalem during the Passover Feast, he performed many other miraculous signs and thousands of Jews witnessed them as a result, Jesus following continued to grow. This, in turn threaten the Pharisees' power even more and made them very nervous, so much so, that one of the leading Pharisees by the name of Nicodemus went to Jesus one dark night so as not to be seen and said, "Rabbi, we know that you are a teacher that comes from God, for no one could perform the miraculous signs that you are doing if God were not with him." Nicodemus was looking for Jesus to give an answer that would reinforce their hold on power, but the answer that Nicodemus would get and take back to the others would deplete their power by giving all of the power to God's one and only Son, Jesus Christ; let's look at the answer that Jesus gave to Nicodemus: "I tell you the truth no one can see the Kingdom of God unless he is born again."

I tell you the truth, no one can enter the Kingdom of God unless he is born of the water and the spirit. Flesh gives birth to the flesh, but the spirit gives birth to the spirit. I tell you the truth, we speak of what we know and we testify to what we have seen, but you people do not accept our testimony." Then Jesus ended His conversation with Nicodemus by relating to him the real heart of the matter, something that Nicodemus could take back to the other

Pharisees. It would be an ending that would let them know exactly where they stood with God, and most importantly, what they had to do in order to change their behavior. Please be guided by Jesus' summary: "For God so loved the world that He gave His only Son, so that whoever believes in Him shall not parish but have eternal life. For God did not send His Son into the world to condemn the world, but to save the world through Him, that whoever believes in Him is not condemned, but whoever does not believe is condemned already, because he has not believed in the name of God's one and only Son." This message that was given to Nicodemus by Jesus was directed straight at the beliefs, teachings and practices of the Pharisees and as such, it only deepened the existing theological abyss between Jesus Christ, the only Son of God and the Pharisees.

To makes matters worse, the Pharisees heard that Jesus was gaining more and more disciples through His teaching and baptizing, even more that John the Baptist. When Jesus learned that The Pharisees knew, He left Judea and went back to Galilee. However, on His way there He had to pass through Samaria. When He got to Samaria, He stopped in a town called Sychar by a well which was located on a plot of land that Jacob had given to his son, Joseph. Jesus was tired from His journey so He sat down by the well to rest, while His disciples went on into town for food. While Jesus was resting, a Samaritan woman came to the well to draw water, seeing her Jesus said to her, "Will you give me a drink?" The Samaritan woman said to Him, "You are a Jew and I am a Samaritan woman, how can you ask me for a drink? (Jews did not associate with Samaritans). It is at this point that I must state that the Samaritan woman was absolutely correct, the Jews hatred and prejudice against the Samarians was very prevalent especially women. But this stop by Jesus was no accident, but was clearly apart of God's redemptive plan. And it is here that I will address the third reason that we, as human beings are biblically separated, that being gender, as mentioned in the beginning of this book. In reading John 4: 1–43, we should pay very close attention to Jesus' actions and to what He is saying to this woman that is so dislike by the Hebrew people. Also, it is worth noting for those who do not know, and for those who want to know, that the Samaritans were describe as people with a high degree of intelligence with a swarty (Dusty Black) complexion. They were the descendents of Nemrod, who was Cush's first son (Cush was the son of Ham). So here we find that Jesus is not only talking to a Samaritan woman, but to a woman who happens to be black. One should also note that Jesus showed absolutely no concern about the prevailing society's rules about talking to Samaritans, especially Samaritan women; His actions proved that. On the other hand, Jesus was in the process of implementing His Father's plan which included every one, meaning every color, every religion and yes, each gender both men as well as women. But let's return to the well where Jesus is continuing His conversation with the Samaritan woman and we find that He is answering her question by saying: "If you knew the gifts of God and who it is that ask you for a drink, you would have asked Him and I would have given you living water." Sir, the woman said, you have nothing to draw with and the well is deep. Where can you get this living water? Are you greater than our father Jacob, who gave us this well and drank from it himself, as did his sons and flocks and herds? Now, with this comment by the Samaritan woman, we now discover that not only are the Samaritans a black race of people as described earlier, but since the Samaritans descended from Jacob, as stated by the Samaritan woman and Jacob was the second son of Isaac (Esau was the first), then genealogy tells us that Jacob, Esau and Isaac were the descendents of Abraham and all were a dark complexioned race of people; and since Abraham and Sarah were the Patriarch and Matriarch, they too must have been of a darker hue. Perhaps you are telling yourself at this point that the bible tells us that Abraham and Sarah were both Hebrews (Jews). Well, you are right. But one Must understand that the first Jews to occupy Jerusalem were called Jebusites, and the Jebusites were or African descent. Also, Jerusalem at the time was known as Jebus. However the name was changed to Jerusalem after King David conquest of this important city. In other words, the ancient Jews were actually descendents from Africa, and just like the thousands of Africans that were brought to the Western World during the slave trade, the Jews' complexion of that time grew lighter over thousands of years due to social assimilation. On the other hand however, for the thousands of black Jews that were abandoned in Ethiopia during that time in history and still remain abandoned today due to their conversion to Christianity, social assimilation was literally void, as a result, these Jews still, to this day, have an extremely dark complexion when it comes to skin tone.

What does all of this mean? It means that the people that we read about in the Old Testament, are people of color and many are as well in the New Testament. If you think back early on in this book, you may remember that Moses, while working for Jethro, the Priest of Median, he met and married Jethro's daughter, Zepporah and they had two children. Also, one should keep in mind that Jethro was a descendent of Cush, and, it was Cush who founded The Land of Cush, which is now called Ethiopia, located in Northeast Africa; Cush was the son of Ham, who was the second son of Noah. So, believe me when I say that the Biblical Moses did not look like Charlton Heston and neither did his wife look like Yvonne DeCarlo!! Again, I repeat, Cecil B. DeMille did an excellent job of telling the story of The Ten Commandments, but he did an injustice to many people of color in his casting for the same movie. And, it has been exactly this type of overall distorted casting in our world, regardless of the type of history being conveyed, that continues to keep us socially ignorant and separated by race. I will say at this time, that during biblical times most of the people that we read about in the Bible are people of color. With that being the case, then color itself was not the problem, however at the time such prejudice did center around Theology, Gender, Economics and/or Power.

As we return to the story, we find that Jesus' responses are creating more and more questions from the Samaritan woman at the well. And one of the following answers given by Jesus did not deviate from this pattern, when Jesus answered: "Everyone that drinks the water that I give them will never thirst again. Indeed, the water that I give them will become in them a spring of water willing up to eternal life."

With this statement by Jesus, He was able to provoke further interest from the woman from Samaria, so much so that the woman did exactly what Jesus knew that she would do, and that is she asked for the water saying: "Sir, give me the water so that I won't get thirsty and keep coming here to draw water." Now that the woman was in a receptive state, Jesus' conversation turned to seeking the truth from this willing soul and when He asked her to go and get her husband and then return, the woman replied: "I have no husband." Then Jesus said to her: "You are right when you say that you have no husband. The fact is, you have had five husbands, and the man you now have is not your husband. So what you have just said is true." It was this revelation about the woman's past that turned her thoughts to the two prevailing theologies during that time, and she said to Jesus: "I can see that you are a prophet. Our fathers worship on this mountain, but you Jews claim that the place that we should worship is in Jerusalem." This statement by the woman now opened the door for Jesus to reveal to her His Father's expectations of how and where one should worship when He responded by declaring: "Believe me woman, the time is coming when you will worship the Father neither on this mountain nor in Jerusalem. For you Samarians worship what you do not know, because salvation is from the Jews. Yet, a time is coming and has now come when the true worshipers will worship the Father in spirit and in truth." With the woman's next comment we are able to see that she has experienced three distinct stages while talking with Jesus, starting with her INTEREST, then her TRUTH and now her FAITH, which is so evident when she states the following: "I know that the Messiah called Christ is coming and when he comes, he will explain everything to us." It was at that point and not a minute before that Jesus revealed Himself to her saying: I WHO SPEAK TO YOU AM HE." So for the very first time, Jesus in a very direct manner tells this Samaritan woman, who by the way is so disliked and so discriminated against, who He actually is. In doing so, Jesus knew in advance that with His disclosure of such news, that He would release the woman from His presence and send her running with excitement without her water jar back into town to give her testimony to the other Samaritans in Samaria. Now let's revisit the gender bias that is in the bible, I agree, it does exist, and I will give you additional examples of such bias further along in this book. But for now, I think that all women should pay particular attention to the behavior of our Lord and Savior, Jesus Christ toward the woman in this story, and when they do they will find that it didn't matter what the society's rules were at that time, it didn't matter what the Hebrew's people's attitudes were toward this woman, and it didn't matter what the Pharisees did or didn't do, because all of their behaviors simply reflected man's imperfections and subsequent sinful ways. The only thing that truly mattered was what Jesus said and did. And, as we continue to advance with our biblical story, all women, as well as all other people who may share their concerns, should continue to pay attention to how Jesus Christ treated all women as oppose to how they were treated and depicted by not only men in the bible, but those who wrote the bible as well. My feeling is, it didn't matter how men acted or what they wrote in the bible about women, what really mattered then and what really matters now is how Jesus Christ treated and continues to treat women, women of all colors and of all religions that he comes in contact with, and I'am including His mother. What this part of our story clearly shows us is that Jesus Christ, by disclosing to the woman at the well who He was, He thereby anointed this woman with the profound knowledge of His earthly existence, and in doing so, she would be only the third person on earth to know, Jesus' mother and His Apostles were the first and second to be told. Nevertheless, to have the knowledge that the Savior of the world actually walks among us and to be able to share such information with others in the form of a testimony, is truly a blessing!

Please be guided by this faith filled, woman from Samaria's testimony to her fellow Samaritans: "You should come and meet the Savior of the world who told me everything that I have done." So when the other Samaritans came to meet Jesus, they urged Him to stay with them, and Jesus stayed for two full days. And because of the words that Jesus Spoke to them, many more became believers. They then said to this woman who ran from Jacob's well with so much faith: "We no longer believe because of what you said, we have heard for ourselves, and we know that this man really is the Savior of the world." When one reads these verses of John in the bible, one must understand that this woman who was such an outcast of the Hebrew society didn't have the same exposure to the teachings passed down from Moses because she was not allowed in the Temple. However in the short time that she spent talking with Jesus at the well, her heart was opened, her faith developed and she believed in Jesus as the Lord and Savior and the only Son of God, and it was because of her faith that Jesus blessed her with the awesome responsibility of announcing His earthly presence.

Now let's move from biblical time and forward on into our times, yes this very day; we find that many women have this same anointing, however many of our religious institutions do not allow women to bring this good news as ministers in their churches. Now when we compare these institutions' actions to that of the Son of God, we are presented with still another opportunity to identify The Pharisees Among Us. We should know as Christians that the examples of Jesus that we read about in the bible, not only served the people in His day, but these examples are a must for us today; you see we only have to look back to our biblical past in order to righteously direct our Christian lives in the future. However, it all depends on whose messages and examples we choose as Christians to follow.

As is stated in first John 30:31, "Jesus performed many other miraculous signs in the presence of His Disciples, which are not recorded in the Bible. But these are written that you may believe that Jesus is the Christ, the Son of

God, and that by believing you may have life in His name. Well, let's look at some of the miracles that were performed by Jesus: the change of water into wine, the miraculous catch of fish, the feeding of five thousand people with only five loaves of bread and two fish, giving sight to the blind, healing the sick, raising the dead, allowing the cripple to walk, the walk on water by Jesus and last but not least, Jesus' death and His resurrection. Now, even with all of these mighty miracles that were performed by Jesus in clear sight for everyone to see, and the more that He explained the proper way to eternal life by believing in Him and the ministry that He was teaching to His Disciples and the thousands of people that now followed Him, the more the Pharisees rose up against Him. So, with each step that Jesus took, the confrontation between Jesus Christ and the Pharisees edged closer and closer. Earlier I alluded to seven distressful reasons that Jesus had to meet with the Pharisees, well let's look at those reasons right now; it appears that Jesus is preaching to his Disciples as well as a large crowd, and He says: "The teachers of the law and the Pharisees sit in Moses' seat. So you must obey them and do everything that they tell you. But do not do as they do, for they do not practice what they preach. They tie up heavy loads and put them on men's shoulders, but they themselves are not willing to lift a finger to move them. Everything that they do is done for men to see them. They make their phylacteries(boxes containing the scripture verses worn on the forehead and arms) wide, and the tassels on their garments long, they also love the place of honor at the banquets and the best seats in the Synagogues, they love to be greeted in the market places and to have men call them Rabbi. But you are not to be called Rabbi, for you have only one Master and you are all brothers. And, do not call anyone on earth father, for you have only one Father and He is in Heaven (so why do we call Catholic Priests fathers instead of Priests). Neither are you to be called teacher, for you have one teacher, the Christ. The greatest among you will be your servant. For whoever exalts himself will be humbled. And whoever humbles himself will be exalted." And now that Jesus had delivered to His Disciples and the large crowds exactly what to do, and exactly what not to do, In His following seven points that He is addressing to the Pharisees, He would explain to them the reasons why.

"THE SEVEN WOES TO THE PHARISEES"

Woe to you teachers of the law and Pharisees, you hypocrites! You shut the Kingdom of Heaven in men's faces. You yourself do not enter, nor will you let those enter who are trying to.

Woe to you teachers of the law and Pharisees, you hypocrites! You travel over land and sea to win a single convert, and when he becomes one you make him twice as much a son of hell as you are. Woe to you blind guides! You say that if anyone swears by the temple it means nothing, but if anyone swears by the gold in the temple, he is bound by his oath. You blind fools!

Which is greater the gold or the temple that makes the gold sacred? Therefore he who swears by the alter, swears by it and by everything on it. And he who swears by the temple swears by it and the one who dwells in it. And he who swears by Heaven, swears by God's throne and by the one who sits on it.

Woe to you teacher of the law and Pharisees, you hypocrites! You give a tenth of your spices, mint, dill and cummin. But you have neglected the more important matters of the law, justice, mercy and faithfulness. You should have practiced the latter without neglecting the former. You blind guides! You strain out a gnat but swallow a camel.

Woe to you teachers of the law and Pharisees, you hypocrites! You clean the outside of the cup and dish, but inside they are full of greed and self-indulgence. Blind Pharisees, first clean the inside of the cup and dish, and then the outside will also be clean. Woe to you teachers of the law and Pharisees, you hypocrites! You are like whitewashed tombs, which looks beautiful on the outside but on the inside are full of dead men's bone and everything unclean. In the same way, on the outside you appear to people as righteous but on the inside you are full of hypocrisy and wickedness.

Woe to you teachers of the law and Pharisees, you hypocrites! You build tombs for the Prophets and decorate the graves of the righteous. And you say if we had lived in the day of our forefathers, we would not have taken part with them in shedding the blood of the Prophets. So you testify against yourselves that you are descendents of those who murdered the Prophets. Fill up then the measure of the sins of your forefathers. In concluding his woeful lecture to the Pharisees, Jesus knew that they didn't believe in him and, more importantly, they didn't want to believe in him, so Jesus left them with a very important message, which for anyone that did not believe in Jesus Christ as the only Son of God, should have paid very close attention to; and it was this: "For I tell you, you will not see me again until you say, blessed is he who comes in the name of the Lord." This message although not very clear to the Pharisees, struck me with a high degree of clarity, and that was, the Pharisees would not see Jesus again until the time had come for them to advocate charges against him. But in order to commit the greatest predestine execution in the history of the world, the Pharisees had to arrange a trap for Jesus which would put him in conflict with the Jewish laws that had been handed down by none other than the Prophet himself, Moses. Now one may ask themselves, how would they be able to accomplished this, well, first of all, they planned to use someone who was the most vulnerable in their society; someone who would have absolutely no rights and no legal recourse to fight such actions. Someone that existed in their unbalanced society, that was forced into sins of the flesh in order to survived and make a living for themselves and their families. And yes, someone that the Pharisees would have known from their own knowledge, exactly where this person would be and exactly what this person would be there for. So the Pharisees conspired to in trap such a person. Now who would such a person happen to be, well, you guessed it! a woman of course. Remember earlier I made the statement, that I agreed that women was treated with much bias in the bible, and that I would point that out later on in this book? Well, the following actions by the Pharisees actually proves my point; You see when Jesus departed from the Pharisees, He continued on with the business of His Father, and that was teaching and converting more and more souls over to His theology. In doing so, Jesus had made His way back to the Temple's court yard and when the people came to hear Him, He started to teach them. The Pharisees and the Teachers of the laws of Moses, in their efforts to conspire against Jesus Christ, brought in this woman who they had caught by trapping her in bed with a man who wasn't her husband. They brought her to the Temple's court yard and made her stand in the middle of this extremely large crowd, in a position of total humility and stark fear. Then the Pharisees said to Jesus: "Teacher, this woman was caught in the act of adultery!! In the law, Moses commanded us to stone such a woman. Now what do you say? But Jesus stopped His teaching and bent down and started to write on the ground with His finger. However the Pharisees continued questioning Him, so He straightened up and said to them; "If any of you is without sin, let him be the first to throw a stone at her." After giving that directive, Jesus bent down again started to write on the ground. Those who heard Him started to have second thoughts, and they started to back away and leave the court yard and soon the rest of them followed. Jesus straightened back up again, turn to the woman and said, "Woman where are they, has anyone condemned you?" "No one sir" she said in a trembling voice "Then neither do I condemn you." "Go now and leave your life of sin."

Clearly this poor woman had sinned, but so had the man that she had sexual relations with....HELLO!! And, as I understand adultery, it is a sexual act between TWO people, so with that being the case, Why didn't the Pharisees bring the man along with the woman to the court yard? Well now, they didn't for the very same reason that I alluded to earlier, that being the extremely strong bias against women. So, as far as I am concerned, the bias against women in the bible is very strongly supported by the contents in the bible itself. But again I must add, for those women who voiced to me their very strong feeling about the way women are treated in the bible and for those who share their concerns, allow me to say that you should be guided by the actions of Jesus Christ toward women in the bible and not those men that practiced such biases. And, in doing so, one should always remember just exactly what the bible is; It is a religious book of history, and it is this history that tells us that God had direct interaction with mankind, while at the same time, this very same history tells us that Jesus Christ, the Son of God, did walk among mankind. So as we study the bible, we should learn from Jesus Christ's examples and from the examples of righteous men, then, incorporate these acts into our lives and live accordingly. On the other hand, we should also learn from the unrighteous acts of man as well, but we should eliminate these types of acts from our lives and don't repeat them. You see, I take issue with those that say don't challenge the bible, because it's a Holy Book. I say yes, the bible is a Holy book, nevertheless, it has unholy people and things in it and these are the people and things that God wants us to challenge, not the book, but some of the people and things in the book. Tell me, how else are we as God's children to learn from this Holy Book called the bible?

As we return to our story, we find that winter has come, and once again Jesus is in the Temple area walking in Solomon's Colonnade. It was also the Feast of Dedication and many Jews had gathered around Jesus, saying, "How long will you keep us in suspense, if you are the Christ, tell us plainly?" (Remember this was exactly what Jesus had done when He spoke with the woman at the well). Well Jesus answered them by stating: "I did tell you, but you do not believe because you are not my sheep. My sheep listen to my voice; I know them and they follow me. With that said, the Jews picked up stones to stone Him, but Jesus said to them, "I have shown you many miracles from the Father, now for which of these do you stone me? The Jews answer reflected their real underlying reason, which was their lack of faith and belief in Jesus Christ, when they said: "We are not stoning you for any of these, but for blasphemy, because you, a mere man, claims to be God.

Again, they tried to seize Him but Jesus escaped their grasp. Now knowing that their patients was growing short, Jesus departed back across the Jordan River where John had been baptizing in the early days. Here Jesus stayed and many people came to see and hear Him. Word among the people was that even John had never preformed a miraculas sign, so his assessment of Jesus' identity was true. And, so while Jesus stayed on the Jordan River, He continued to teach, and in the process, He converted thousands of people.

However, while Jesus was going about His Father's work, Lazarus, who was a very dear friend of Jesus, became very ill. Now Lazarus along with his wife Martha and his sister Mary Magdelene lived in a town called Bethany. It was the sister that had sent word to Jesus that the one that He loved was sick. When Jesus heard this, He said: "This sickness will not end in death. No, it is for God's glory so that His Son may be glorified through it." Now it was very well known that Jesus loved Lazarus as well as his sister, Mary. Nevertheless, when Jesus got the word that his friend Lazarus was sick, He continued to stay where He was for two days. Then, on the third day He said to His disciples, "Let's go to Judea." But Rabbi they answered, a short time ago the Jews tried to stone you, and yet you are going back there? At that point, Jesus went on to tell them that their friend has fallen asleep; but I'am going there to wake him up. His disciples, still worried about the dangers in Judea, replied to Jesus, "Lord if he is asleep he will wake up." You see, in the minds of the disciples they were talking about a natural state of sleep, however Jesus was referencing another one of his mighty miracles. Now, it was this lack of understanding by the male disciples of Jesus that reminded me all throughout this story, time and time again, that most of the men did not display the same esoterical knowledge of Jesus' meanings as did the women disciples, including the other women that met and talked to the Son of God. As a matter of fact, Mary Magdalene oftentimes would have to explain the true meaning of Jesus' teachings to the male disciples, including Peter. As a result of this esoterical knowledge of Jesus' teachings possessed by women in the Bible, Jesus could therefore speak to them in a very direct manner, because the knowledge that they had emanated from the deep rooted faith that was in their hearts. On the other hand, the male disciples' faith most of the time was shaky to say the least, and, what emanated from such shaky faith was the inability to comprehend much of what Jesus was teaching. It was because of this lack of understanding that Jesus finally had to explain to his male disciples that Lazarus, their dear friend had died. Then he further explained that Lazarus death was for their sake. Also, Jesus went on to say that he was glad that he was not there so that they may believe what he was about to do. Jesus then said "Let's go to him." So in order to prove their love for Jesus, Thomas called to the rest of the disciples, "let's us go also, that we may die with him." Upon their arrival, Jesus found out that Lazarus had been dead for four days. Also, with Bethany being less than two miles from Jerusalem, many Jews had come to comfort the family. Martha, Lazarus' wife went out to meet Jesus, but Mary, Lazarus' sister, stayed behind at their home. When Martha met Jesus, she said to him, "If you had been here Lord, my husband would not have died. But, I know even now God will give you whatever you ask." Once again this woman's statement not only proves her very strong faith in Jesus Christ, but it also tells us that she fully understands the relationship between God the Father and God the Son. Hearing her strong faith demonstrated, Jesus then said: "Your husband will rise again." But Martha, expressing her faith in the teachings of Jesus stated: "I know that he will rise again come the resurrection of the last day." Jesus then said to her: "I am the resurrection and the life, he who believes in me will live, even though he dies, and he that lives and believe in me will never die." Now seeking to confirm her faith and understanding once again, Jesus said to her, "Do you believe this?" "Yes Lord said Martha I believe that you are the Christ, the only Son of God who has come into this world." Here again, we find yet another woman testifying as to her total faith in Jesus Christ as the Son of God. And, once again in my research of the scriptures, it became very clear to me that women during Biblical times, be they Samaritan women or Jewish women, over and over again, they exhibited a much stronger faith in the theology taught by Jesus Christ; certainly much more than the men in the society. It would appear that as a result of their faith, a strong spiritual relationship between the women in the society and Jesus was developed more quickly, and it was because of this very deep faith that was exemplified by women, that Jesus' communications were received by them in a clear and distinct manner. Men on the other hand, had a harder time both in understanding and truly accepting Jesus, so their faith was slow in coming and extremely inconsistent. Now because Jesus could see into men's heart, Jesus' communications with them were of a testing nature. Even his male disciples that followed him, the very ones that he had spent so much time teaching, demonstrated at times their very weak faith.

Let us review First John, 14:9, Jesus' arrest is imminent and he is preparing his disciples for his departure, when Philip, still not understanding and shaky about his beliefs, ask Jesus to show them the father so that they may feel secure when he left. Jesus responded to Philip's request by saying: Don't you know me Philip, Even after I have been among you for such a long period of time? Anyone who has seen me has seen the Father. So, how can you say show us the Father?" It was this difference between men's faith and the women's faith, while writing this book that told me that in order for Christ to penetrate one's soul depends first of all, on one's ability to let him in. So maybe, just maybe, this was the reason that God chose the woman Mary for His Son to be born into this world. I truly feel that God's decision truly reflects the love and deep respect that He holds for women in general; which by the way, is the very same love and respect that is shared by His Son, Jesus Christ.

AND, EVEN THOUGH GOD MADE WOMAN FROM THE BODY OF A MAN, STILL, MAN CANNOT ENTER INTO THIS WORLD, EXCEPT THROUGH THE BODY OF A WOMAN, AS DID GOD'S ONLY SON, JESUS THE CHRIST.

OH! OH!............WHAT A JUST GOD IT IS THAT WE SERVE!!

We find that when Martha had finished speaking with Jesus, she returned home and told her sister-in-law that Jesus had ask for her, after hearing this, Mary left the house quickly to meet with Jesus and all of the Jewish people that had gathered in the family's home, also left quickly right behind Mary, because they thought that she was returning to the tomb to continue mourning. But instead, Mary went to meet with Jesus. When Mary saw Jesus, she fell to her knees and said: "Lord if you had been here my brother would not have died." When Jesus saw that she was weeping and so were the people that had followed her out to meet with Him, He was deeply moved and troubled. Jesus asked, "Where have you laid him." Before Mary could respond, the crowd shouted, come and see Lord! As Jesus turned to follow the crowd and Mary to the tomb, He felt the pain of their loss and the sorrow of their tears, and so Jesus wept. When they came to the tomb, Jesus saw that the opening was covered with a large round stone. He said, "Take away the stone." Mary replied, "But Lord, by now there is a bad odor, for he has been dead for four days." Then Jesus answered, "Did I not tell you that if you believe, you would see the glory of God?' So they rolled away the stone. Then Jesus looked up and said, "Father, I thank you that you have heard me. I know that you always hear me, but I said this for the benefit of people standing here, that they may believe that you sent me." Now even at that moment and time, Jesus saw this as an opportunity to further convert more Jewish people by glorifying His Father in fulfilling the purpose that he sent him to accomplish. Then Jesus said in a very loud voice, "Lazarus! Come out." And with that demand, the man that was dead came walking out. His hands and feet were wrapped in strips of linen, with a cloth that covered his face. Jesus then instructed them to take off the grave clothes and let him go. Seeing this, many of the Jewish people that had come to be with the grieving family in time of need, put their faith in Jesus and some went back and told the Pharisees exactly what Jesus had done. After hearing this latest report on Jesus' accomplishment, The Chief Priest and the Pharisees called a meeting of the Sanhedrin. "What are we accomplishing? they asked. "Here is this man performing many miraculous signs. If we allow him to go on like this, everyone will believe in him and the Romans will come and take away both our place of power and our nation." Now it was this statement by the Pharisees that clearly demonstrated the fact that they considered Jesus a threat to their positions among the Hebrew people, even though they knew who Jesus was; they were more concerned about their power being eroded. So, it was the High Priest Caiaphas who spoke up and said, "You should realize that it is better for one man to die for the people, than for the whole nation to parish." With that statement, the predictable death of Jesus Christ was sealed, but this statement would also free not only the Hebrew nation, but all other nations from the original sin that have haunted our lives due to the fall of our first parents, Adam and Eve. You see the consequences of Jesus' death means that our original sin will be replaced with our free will, therefore giving mankind the choice to determine where we will choose to spend our eternal lives, based on our belief or lack of belief in Jesus Christ as the one and only Son of God. Nevertheless, because of God's power and grace which continued to be manifested through His Son Jesus Christ, the Pharisees from that day forward became more active in their attempts to have Jesus brake the laws of Moses so that they could put Jesus to death using the Roman Government as their executioner. Because Jesus time had not yet come, He no longer moved among the Hebrew people.

So, Jesus withdrew to a place called Ephraim, there He stayed with His disciples. And when it was time for the Jewish Passover, many left the country side and went into Jerusalem for their ceremonial cleansing before the Passover. Everyone kept looking for Jesus as they stood in the Temple area, also they were asking each other if Jesus was coming to the feast, not knowing that the Pharisees had given orders that if anyone found out where Jesus was, then he or she should report it so that they may arrest him. In the meantime, some six days before Passover, Jesus arrived at Lazarus' house, the man that He had raised from the dead. There a dinner was given in Jesus' honor, Martha served the dinner while Lazarus relaxed and talked with Jesus and His disciples. Meanwhile, Mary took the time to get about a pint of nard, which was a very expensive perfume. On the other hand, a very large crowd found out that Jesus was at Lazarus' home and they began pouring in around Lazarus' house to see both Jesus and Lazarus. Now when the Chief Priest found out where Jesus was, he made plans to kill not only Jesus, but Lazarus as well, his thinking was, it because of Lazarus being raised from the dead that many Jewish people were converting over to Jesus and putting their faith in Him. Also, just for the record, there were some Jewish people in leadership positions that did believe in Jesus, however they were afraid that if they confessed their faith in Jesus Christ, the Pharisees would put them out of the Synagogue. So here we see yet another example of the men's shaky faith and their inability to act.

Again, the men in the society never exhibited that strong backbone of faith that was exemplified by many of the women in the same society, when they themselves spoke to Jesus and testified to their faith. As a matter of fact, the men in general appeared to be more concerned about their leadership positions and the power that they wielded in the society, rather than being concerned about their faith and what Jesus was teaching. I must also admit that the more that I evaluated the reactions of the men to Jesus Christ during biblical times, and then compare their reactions to that of women during the same time period, I had to wonder while doing the research for this book, exactly what would I be writing about had women been in the positions of leadership and power and, as a result, ran the societies and enforced the laws? Well now, that is a very good question, and maybe it is a question that I should address in what could be a completely different book!! But, if I did decide to write such a book and based my research solely on the bible, then the story would be somewhat limited, because there is limited information about women available; or is there? This too is another book!!!

It is really for this very same reason that I became an author, because like women, as an African American man, I realized early on that it has been someone else's version(s) that has always defined my race of people throughout history, and in almost all cases, these same versions have omitted our real contributions.

And, their descriptions of our accomplishments or lack of accomplishments, have been inaccurate and in many cases, still remain inaccurate to this day. It was for this reason that when I started writing this book, I prayed to God that he would bless me, first of all with the wisdom, and then with the skills to accurately define the true achievements of all of God's people and this does include Black people as well; so that for all of the people that will read this book, may they fully understand the contributions of all people of color, be they people that lived during biblical times, or people of color presently. This includes those that came before me, my ancestors, as well as those that will come after me, my descendents. For it is then and only then that people all over the world will understand and appreciate the total achievements and contributions made to this world by all people of color. In order to accomplish this, I felt very comfortable starting at the point that it all began, and that is with the world's very first history book, the Bible. This effort represents my second book in this area of history. So, now I will continue on with this phase of that same history, "The Pharisees among Us." As we return to the story, we now find that the Passover Feast was very near and Jesus knew that his time had come for him to leave this world and return to his Father. But first there were more examples that he wanted to set for his disciples. So, with this thought in mind, he stood up from the meal that they were having and removed his outer clothing and then he wrapped a towel around his waist. Jesus then told his disciples that no servant was greater than his master, nor is a messenger greater than the one that sent him. Jesus continued, now that you know These things, you will be blessed if you do them. Jesus not forgetting his Father's plan, went on to put into motion both of his betrayals which first he COMMANDED of Judas, then he inserted his second COMMAND directed at Peter's three time denial. At this point it is extremely important to understand that neither of these loyal servants acted out of a prophecy, but from commands that was given by Jesus to them and each of these commands were given based on each disciples' respective ability to carry out such commands. You see if Peter and Judas had not done their parts, then they would have been put to death along with Jesus; this was something that could not happen.

The commands given to Peter and Judas would allow the Christian movement started by Jesus for his Father to continue long after he had departed. However, now the accountability will belong to the Holy Spirit to instruct the disciples. With this in mind, Jesus recognized that the disciples were becoming more and more concern about his departure, so, in order to address their concerns, Jesus spoke in John 14: 1–4, here Jesus said the following: "Do not let your hearts be troubled. Trust in God, trust also in me. For in my Father's house are many rooms, if it was not so, I would have told you. And I will go there and prepare a place for you, I will return and take you with me, so that where ever I am, there you will be also. You know the place that I am going." Hearing this, one of the disciples named Thomas again reflected both his lack of understanding and faith when he said: "Lord, we don't know where you are going, so how could we know the way." Jesus then answered: "I am the way the truth and the life. No one comes to the Father except through me." Still, after these instructions the disciples were feeling very low and afraid; for who would now be their counselor when they needed guidance. It was then for the first time that Jesus announced the coming of the Holy Spirit, the third person of the Holy Trinity. And now for all of those people that didn't believe in the second person of the Holy Trinity, that being the Son of God, they would fall further behind in their efforts of faith because now they would have a spirit imbedded deep within them that the world around them would not ever be able to see or hear. Nevertheless, with Jesus' explanation to the disciples we will now get an opportunity to discover exactly how the Holy Spirit will be manifested in the lives of the disciples as well as in all others people who believe when Jesus said: "If you love me you will do what I command. And I will ask the Father, and He will give you another counselor to be with you forever, the Spirit of truth. The world cannot accept him, because it neither sees him or knows him. But you know him, for he lives with you and will be in you. I will not leave you as orphans; I will come to you." Jesus then told his disciples that He was telling them this while He was with them, but when he departed, His Father would send a counselor, The Holy Spirit in His name, and the Holy Spirit will teach them all things and would remind them of everything that He had said to them. Also, the peace that was given to the disciples by Jesus was not the same peace that would be given by the world. So, do not let your hearts be trouble and do not be afraid. Jesus also explained to the disciples that they would experience grief, but, their grief would turn to joy just as a woman giving birth to a child has pain, but when her child is born she forgets the anguish because of her joy that her child is born into the world. Here, once again, we have a chance to witness Jesus' empathy of the physical pain as well as emotional joy that God has bestowed upon women through the miracle of child birth; and now Jesus uses this God given miracle of child birth to exemplify to His disciples the joy of His pending resurrection; and it is His death and resurrection that Jesus was thinking about when He then looked toward Heaven and prayed for Himself. Then He prayed for His disciples and for all of the believers. When Jesus had finished praying, He left with His disciples and they crossed the Kidron Valley. On the other side of this valley was an olive grove, and it was there that Jesus and His disciples went in to rest. However by this time Judas had betrayed Jesus for thirty pieces of silver that was paid to him by the Pharisees. Judas, knowing the place that Jesus and the disciples would be resting, told this to Jesus' pursuers. As a result of Judas' information, a detachment of soldiers and some officials from the Chief Priest and the Pharisees was on their way, being guided by none other than Judas himself. Darkness had fallen and the crowd that was looking for Jesus was carrying torches, lanterns and weapons. With Jesus knowing all that was to happen to Him, He proactively went out to meet with them, and as they approached and was in speaking distance, it was Jesus that asked: "Who is it that you want?" They replied, "Jesus of Nazareth." Knowing that His time had now come, Jesus for the very first time when conversing with men, answered them with a very direct response when He said: "I am he." It is here that I must answer the question of who actually killed Jesus, was it the Jews or was it the Romans? Well, since the answer has rested in the bible for thousands of years, let's explore the facts, as such historical facts are recorded in the bible itself; when we do, we will find that it was the Romans that killed Jesus Christ, but, not without the complicity of the Jewish leadership. Just as when we examine the history of slavery in the western world, we will find that slavery was initiated and executed by Whites, but not without the complicity of some African Tribal leaders for personal gain. *Nevertheless, when one examine both the actions of the Jews, as well as the Romans, the following is what one will conclude: The Jews, once they found out the purpose for which Jesus was born into this world (and they did know), they stalk Him; they continually tried to trick Him by quoting the laws that were handed down from Moses and they compared such laws to Jesus' teaching. They tried to have Him stoned, They even tried to have Jesus pronounce stonning upon others, the accused Him of breaking the laws on the Sabbath, and, they even bribed another Jew by offering him thirty pieces of silver and culminated with his kiss of betrayal. Last but not least, These same Jews continually demanded, time and time again the death of Jesus while He was in the custody of the Roman ruler, eventhough the Roman ruler at the time was willing to give Jesus His freedom, and had tryed several times to do just that. However, each time the Roman ruler tryed to release Jesus he was met with extremely strong opposition by the Pharisees. All in all, the Jewish Men that were in leadership positions at the time, were very successful in their efforts to offer a prosecutorial case against Jesus. The Roman leader on the other hand, eventhough reluctant, was, in the end, just as poroficient in his efforts to execute the only son of God, Jesus Christ. Now, as Chriatian on whom should we place the blame? Well, we can blame but we cannot judge, because God has told us that He will do that. However, all of us should be aware of what Jesus' sentiments were at the time about His sentence in the most important death penalty case ever recorder in world history.*

The reason why one should be aware of this type of crucifixion as a form of death is because as human beings, history continues to tell us that when we are kept ignorance about the negative socially advocated deaths in our societies, or we simply choose not to remember, then we as human beings have a tendency to repeat them. Let's take a realistic look at our history, weather that history is the eighteenth, nineteenth or twentieth century. And when one view such history, one will then find that there have been many crucifixions repeated, and yes trees were use also, but, instead of nails to affix the victims to the trees, ropes were used to hang them from one of the strong branches of the trees. And many times when ropes were not used to facilitate the death of victims, such ropes were used as a reminder of death, in order to frighten and intimidate an entire race of people. Also, instead of a spear to the side to expedite death, razors were used to castrate these black victims, especially when such victims were accused of looking at women of the white race, the wrong way, at the wrong time. Then there have been black men that have been tied to the bumpers of pickup trucks and dragged down highways until their skin was peeled off and death ensued, or a gay man that was beaten to death out of pure ignorance about his life style, then left hanging of a fence along a country road just like the crosses were left on the hill of Calvary on the roads that led from the city, all of this was done in ancient times and in our times so that all could see what some in the respective communities thought about such life styles. Now I have tried very hard not to draw a correlation between the Jewish people and the Roman Government during ancient times to our private citizens and State Governments today in the way they have put innocence people to death, but, that correlation does exist! Nevertheless, I thank my dear God every single day for an attorney by the name of Mr. Berry Scheck, of The Innocence Project, the FORENSIC DNA process that they have perfected have freed many, many people from prison after long periods served on death row, most importantly, these same people lives were saved for crimes they did not commit, just as the

Is Garrett the only choice?

Tim Cowlishaw: In this coaching competition, the incumbent is miles ahead of the rest. SPORTSDAY, 1C

The Dallas Morning News

Leading Newspaper $1.00   Dallas, Texas, Tuesday, January 4, 2011   news®

DNA clears 2 in 1979 Dallas rape, robbery

DALLAS COUNTY

DNA clears 2 in '79 rape, robbery

Men have served 30 years; evidence from older cases a surprise

By JENNIFER EMILY
Staff Writer
jemily@dallasnews.com

Two men convicted in connection with a 1979 Dallas rape, robbery and abduction have been cleared of the crime

through DNA testing. They have served about three decades in prison — more than any other Texas inmate cleared by DNA testing.

The exonerations are also the first where DNA testing has been used in Dallas County to prove men innocent of crimes that occurred as far back as the 1970s. Until recently, authorities thought that evidence had

only been preserved by the county's crime lab since 1981, said Nina Morrison of the Innocence Project in New York. The discovery that other testable evidence exists could mean Dallas County's national record number of 20 exonerations since 2001 will keep growing.

"It may provide grounds to go back and look at other evi-

dence from older cases where we thought there was nothing to test," Morrison said. "It's really a miracle it was saved."

Cornelius Dupree Jr., 51, is expected to be exonerated today in a Dallas County courtroom. He is on parole after having been released in July. He spent more than 30 years in prison.

See **DNA** Page 4A

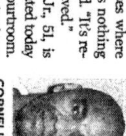

CORNELIUS DUPREE JR. was released on parole in July.

ANTHONY MASSINGILL will remain in prison for now.

innocent Jesus Christ died for crimes he did not commit. So, if we as a society are still committing the same acts as did the Pharisees and Romans, then I truly see no difference in our cultures, as a matter of fact, I would even say that the Pharisees as well as the Romans are still among us!!

Many Christians and Non-Christians alike have speculated about how Jesus Christ really felt about the degree of guilt between the Jewish Pharisees and the Roman rulers; well now, let's allow Jesus himself to explain to us exactly how he felt, and we can do just that by going to the book of John 19: 10–11, here one will become very much aware of how Jesus felt about the degree of guilt between the Pharisees and the Roman Government. Let's review, you see Pilate had just been informed by the Pharisees that Jesus had yet again broken another Jewish law which was punishable by death. Armed with this new information, Pilate was even more concerned when he returned to question Jesus. Pilate asked Jesus, "Where do you come from?" But Jesus gave no answer. Do you refuse to speak to me Pilate responded. Don't you realize that I have the power to free you, or to have you crucified?" We now learn Jesus' true feelings about the degree of guilt when the Son of God says the following: "You would have no power over me if it were not given to you from above. THEREFORE, THE ONES THAT HANDED ME OVER TO YOU ARE GUILTY OF A GREATER SIN." So you see it was this explanation by Jesus to Pilate that tells us about Jesus' exact feelings. Now what Jesus was explaining to Pilate was this: Pilate's sin which was yet to come, was a sin, but it would be made out of ignorance and his eventual decision for Jesus' death would be apart of God's overall plan for his Son to depart this world. Now, as for the Jewish people that plotted and conspired to hand Jesus over for execution, well they were guilty of a greater sin, because they did so in order to hold on to their power even though they had full knowledge of Jesus' true identity. So, with our story drawing to the expected end, we will see the arrest of Jesus; an arrest in which he is beaten as a form of punishment before, during and after his trial, even on his way up the hill to Calvary. On the way there however, Jesus fell some seven times under the weight of this cross that he was made to carry on his beaten and bloody shoulders. After the seventh fall, Jesus was too weak to sustain the weight of the cross, so he was assigned the help of a large North African man of color from Cryene. Now here again, I find it ironically misleading that some people believe that people of color, especially black people, who were supposed to have been cursed because of the sin of Ham, and as a result they were excluded from the Bible and any interactions with Jesus Christ. This is not true, the Bible does not mention people by race (Jews being the exception) because the Bible is not a book about race. Nevertheless, the North African man of color from Cryene is yet another example that such interactions did take place and takes place all throughout the Bible. Remember, when one studies the Bible and not just read it, it is very important to do the following: 1). Determine WHO you are studying about, 2). Determine WHAT you are studying about and 3). Determine WHERE the events that you are studying about took place, as such places relate to the world's current geography.

Continuing on, we find that while Jesus struggled on the way to the place of his execution, he was followed by his Mother Mary, his brother James and his most favorite disciple, Mary Magdalene. Missing from this following are the rest of his disciples because they were afraid that their presence would mean their deaths as well. This was not the case however with Mary Magdalene, you see she had faith and took Jesus at his word when he said: "Do not be afraid I will be with you even until the end of time." Now I make this point only to point out that as humans, we, in many cases, fear the world's vengeance more than we believe in God's promised protection as spoken by his Son, Jesus Christ. Again, a quick note about the faith and strength of women in the Bible, you see this was not the first time that the disciple Mary Magdalene risked her life out of concern for her Lord and Savior, Jesus the Christ, as we will discover with the continuance of this story.

With the death of Jesus, many have said that He died much too young at thirty three years of age, but I say that He died complete, because He completed every single act that God, His Father in heaven wanted Him to complete. In addition, it is because of His death and subsequent resurrection, that death itself have been defeated and we are offered the salvation of eternal life. We also find that after Jesus' death, His body was removed from the cross, treated and placed in a tomb, afterwhich a large stone was rolled over the opening of the tomb. While this was going on, the Apostles continued to remain in hiding, fearing that they would be next to be crucified. However, this was not the fear of a young woman by the name of Mary Magdalene. What many of us may, or may not know, is that Mary Magdalene had spent more time with Jesus than any other Apostles. She was extremely faithful and her understanding of Jesus' teachings was seen as esoterical. As a matter of fact, many times she would have to explain the meaning of Jesus' teachings to the other Apostles, including Peter. And, as a result of her intelligent understanding and faithful relationship with Jesus, some of the Apostles had named her the beloved Disciple, because they thought that Jesus loved her more than any of them. Also, because of Mary's very close relationship with Jesus, she had been seen with Jesus almost every place that He traveled, so she was very well known by many people as one of the disciples that preached and associated with this person that the Pharisees called a spiritual trouble maker. So the Pharisees knew her very well. It is my true feeling as a result of my religious research, that Mary Magdalene was Jesus' head disciples (read The Gospel of Mary, written by Ester A. De Boer). But, because the Bible was both recorded and edited by men, and because those men that were in power did an effective job of completely discrediting Mary's life, subsequently more important information about Mary Magdalene's spiritual responsibilities was not included in the Bible. This is a void in which the Catholic Church recently apologized for the part that they played in this historical distorted action. What is documented however is the fact that there were many other women that followed Jesus Christ, and the duties that they performed were different, based on each woman's talents. For example, some did the washing, cooking, sewing, ect...While there were others like Mary Magdalene that financed Jesus' ministry and conducted spiritual duties that were the same as the male disciples. Apart from Mary, there were Joanna, the wife of Chuza, Herod's steward, as well as a lady by the name of Susanna, and still there were others. As a matter of fact, Jesus depended on Mary Magdalene more than any of his other disciples and he had ordained her to carry on as the natural leader of his Father's Christian movement long after he had departed. However, to elaborate on this would take me into another book, a book that I intend to write in the not too distant future, but not now.

As we return to our story, we find that Mary Magdalene's actions shows that she had more concern for the body of Jesus Christ than she had for her own safety; even though she, like all other women that lived in the society at that time, actually had no rights, and as a result, they were more at risk of punishment, or even death than were men in that same society. Now that we understand the prevailing culture, we still find that Mary, early that Sunday morning on the third day after Jesus' death, was on her way to the tomb, still, as a matter of fact, not fearing any consequences, neither was she looking for places to hide on the way like the disciples that were hiding behind locked doors. After Mary arrived at the tomb she noticed that the large round stone that had covered Jesus' tomb had been rolled away and when she looked inside she discovered that the tomb was empty. Now fearing that the Romans had taken Jesus' body away, Mary paniced, turned and ran as fast as she could back to where the other disciples were hiding. Upon her hurried arrival, Mary, while still short of breath, spoke to them in a very urgent voice. She informed them that the body of Jesus had been removed. The disciples, their faces reflecting even more fear, left their place of hiding, running one behind the other not saying a word along the way. When they arrived, they too looked inside the tomb only to find it empty. Now fearing the concern that Jesus had voiced to both Peter and Judas, they anticipated that their own deaths were even more imminent, so they again turned and ran as fast as they could back into hiding behind locked doors. Left alone, Mary Magdalene fell to her knees in tears, now sadden even more by the missing body of Jesus the Christ. Jesus, seeing her love and devotion for and to him, a love which was absent of fear, made his first direct appearance to mankind after his death. In studying this biblical event, one must understand that Jesus could have appeared at any time while the rest of the disciples were there at the grave site with Mary, but he did not; instead, he chose to address Mary when she was alone, and after his conversation with her, he then chose to anoint Mary Magdalene, this young beautiful woman who's life was so disrespected, so dishonored and publicly distorted by a male dominated society to deliver the earth shattering news to his disciples that his predicted resurrection was now true. As Christians, we should understand the real significance of the resurrection of our Lord and Savior, Jesus Christ, because it is this act by God that distinguishes Christianity from all other forms of religions. And just think, our biblical history tells us that this earth shattering news was given first of all to a Woman to be delivered to men who were hiding behind lock doors fearing for their lives. Well now, this was the second time such earth shattering news was given to a woman, remember the Samaritan woman at the well? Biblical incidents like these should tell all people all over the world exactly how God through his Son, Jesus Christ, loves women and respect their abilities to lead not only during Biblical times but in our times as well. For those churches and/or institutions in our current societies that haven't learn what the Bible has been instructing us to do for centuries, I would say that such churches and institutions continues to defy the teachings of our Lord and Savior, Jesus Christ by their pharisaical actions.

Here once again we see yet another example of Jesus' relationship with women and his respect for them, which again differed greatly from the prevailing male dominated society at that time. What biblical history tells us is because of Mary Magdalene's faith, love and lack of concern for her own safety, Jesus recognized her as the leader that would carry his Christian movement forward, so Jesus Christ, the only Son of God, anointed Mary Magdalene, the disciple that he so very much loved and the disciple that so very much understood his teachings with being the first human being on earth to proclaim his resurrection; and Jesus sent her to not only carry this message to the rest of the disciples but to the rest of the world. When Jesus' life on this earth came to an end, it also marked the end of his battles with the Pharisees and those other people in the society who followed their way of thinking. So, it is at this point that I should pause and determine if, in this story, I have explain the concerns that were raised in the beginning of this book, and they were: THE BIBLE HAS SEPARATED US BY RACE, BY GENDER AND BY RELIGION. First what did we determine about race? Well for one thing, we know that the Bible is not a book about race, nevertheless this well known history book does have a diverse race of people in it, including Africans, which by the way is the land/territory where the Bible begins. Even though such geographical information is not fully explained in the Bible(Ethiopia is referred to as the Land of Cush) with the proper geographical coherency so that we may identify the different lands/territories as they exist today, still, too many of our religious institutions, ministers and institutional scholars continues to remain silent for whatever reason(s) to establish this fact; a fact that when discovered would dismiss our ignorance in this and many other areas of the Bible. Continuing, we now know that Ham, identified as the second son of Noah, was a black man of color who was not cursed and neither were his descendents. Allow me to justify my claim. You see one must remember that the Caananites were descendents of Caanan and not Ham, because as we are told in Genesis 9: 24–27, that Noah identified Caanan, his youngest son as the one that sinned against him and as a result, it was Caanan that Noah cursed. As for Ham and his descendents, well, they were instead blessed and they migrated to other lands throughout Africa and Asia as per God's instructions to go forth, be fruitful and multiply. And it was Ham and Ham's descendents that built many strong, rich societies and these societies contributed greatly to a new and rapidly growing world. We also know that Ham was born a man of color and not turned that way because of a curse, as some German religious scholars have advocated. And, since Ham was born a person of color, then so were his other two brothers, Shem and Japheth because each of them came from the union of one man, Noah and one woman, Noah's wife. Now if this be the case, then utilizing the intellect that God has given us, one can draw the conclusion that both Noah and his wife were people of color as well. Now let's evaluate the second concern, that being Gender. Did this story arrest the concerns of those, including myself, who feel that women are both disrespected and discriminated against in this first book of history called the Bible? Allow me to say that the word arrest is much too strong of a word, simply because one cannot go back in history and arrest events that, at the time, continued to exist. You may ask why? Well my answer to that question is this, it cannot be arrested for the same reason that we cannot currently arrest the practice of racial discrimination in our society today, because it continue to exist!!

However, the bible does give us example to follow when it comes to the welfare and treatment of women not only in the Bible but in our current society as well. We can find such examples when we focus on the life of Jesus Christ when He walked on this earth. You see, Jesus never disrespected or discriminated or damned any woman regardless of who or what those women were. On the contrary, when we witness Jesus' interactions with women in the bible, He not only talked to women in public and was touched by women in public, which by the way was against the Hebrew laws, no, the laws that Jesus followed was that of His Father in Heaven, which was totally opposite of mankind's laws at that time and still is today. We must always remember That Jesus went so far as to anoint some women to carry forth His Father's message as articulated by Him to others, therefore assuring that to those who would listen, they would have a path to heaven through Jesus Christ and not a direct path to God via the laws. Thirdly, did this book explain the reason as to why we, the very people that were created by God Himself, yet we are separated by the preceived theologies presented in this timeless history book called the Bible. Well let's review the construction of the Bible and what this construction actually tells us. When we do this we will find that God has a two part plan in the Bible which is intended solely for our eternal salvation. Now in Plan (A) the New Testament, we will find that God interacted with mankind directly, testing each of the persons that He interacted with by assigning them duties based on the talents that He had given to them. For example, Abraham was given the responsibility of organizing God's chosen people into tribes, and by example teaching them how to be righteous in the eyes of God. In the process, God appointed Abraham to become the father of all nations. God also interacted directly with the Prophets through visionary communications, as a result, these Prophets were able to deliver to the people God's wishes along with the predictions that God had shared with them. And then there was Moses, born a Hebrew but raised an Egyptian, Moses was selected by God because of his leadership, his sense of justice and most of all Moses' compassion for people in general. And, in reading the book of Exodus, one can clearly see that it took all of these qualities and then some for Moses to effectively lead God's people out of bondage in Egypt. An important but often time misunderstood strategy by God was that He saw that the world was leaderless, lawless and very sinful, so God gave Moses the additional responsibility of introducing and implementing laws and decrees that would bring social order to former slaves who had never before govern themselves. Nevertheless, these over six hundred laws and decrees were for their social order and not given as a pathway to God as many believed then and some still believe today.

On the other hand, it would take some forty years for the children of Israel to become accustom to governing themselves utilizing God's laws, after which, Joshua and not Moses would lead them into the Promise Land after the successful battle of Jericho. Now, because God interacted directly with mankind and setup laws which were initiated through human channels, some people and some groups, even some religions therefore believed that salvation was, and is now, through God Himself. In other words, if such people therefore kept God's laws, then these laws would be sufficient to get them to Heaven. As a result, for those people or institutions that practiced this belief, they really had no need for anything that is in the bible beyond the Old Testament, or as I've described it, Plan (A). Of course it is this myopic view within this theological practice that actually separates God's Plan (A), from God's Plan (B). So, let's examine Plan (B), and when we do, one will see that the strategy offered therein was and is different and for good reasons, you see the world during the time of the New Testament was different. For one thing the world had matured, there were laws that govern the society, there were places to worship, market places for food and businesses, schools had been established, and yes, even taxes were being collected. As a result, God no longer worked His will directly through mankind, but instead He assign all future communications and teachings over to His Son, Jesus Christ who He dispatched to earth manifested as man, and it would be through Him not the laws, that the stain of original sin would be lifted from our souls and our eternal salvation would be dictated by mankind's free will. No one knows just how many duties that God assigned to His Son, but judging from Jesus' accomplishments, they were many. However, I can attest to the main three, and they were and still are: Forgiveness, Redemption and the Grace of God through His Son, Jesus Christ. It was these three assigned duties that are still the very essence of the theology that was taught by Jesus Christ. And, after teaching these duties during the time that He walked this earth, He then gave up His life, which in turn, finalized the forgiveness of the original sin that we are all born into this world with. But for those people or those religious institutions that are still resisting the correct way to acquire eternal salvation with God, they should be guided by these words from Jesus Christ Himself when He stated in John 14: verse 6: "I AM THE WAY THE TRUTH AND THE LIFE. NO ONE COME UNTO THE FATHER EXCEPT THROUGH ME." It is this very clear proclamation by Jesus Christ that stands in direct conflict with those who believe that it is the law or their deeds that will earn them a direct path to God. Additionally, it is this proclamation by Jesus in the above verse that stands as the separating factor between people and religious institutions.

As mentioned earlier, after the death of Jesus Christ, we have the opportunity in Plan (B) to witness the assignment of a new accountability that emerged on earth when Jesus requested from His Father the Holy Spirit, and upon Jesus' Request, God sent the counseling of the Holy Spirit and even though the world could not see him or hear him, still, he would be buried deep in our souls and from there he would instruct and guide our lives according to the teachings of Jesus Christ. This story tells us that when God assigned accountabilities to each of the persons that he interacted with, there were no overlapping of responsibilities; for example, after Abraham's responsibilities ended, there was Moses, after Moses, came Joshua, after Joshua, came King David, after King David, Jesus Christ, after Jesus Christ, came the Holy Spirit. It was this type of ascension plan by God that tells us that God had a plan then, and he has a plan now. The question is, how many of us realize that we are now apart of his plan, and as such, we are accountable. If we are to facilitate God's Kingdom here on earth, as in the prayer that he has ask us to pray, then it will be in how we treat and relate to each other; remember Jesus' request to Peter: Peter, if you love me feed my sheep (my people). Then, Peter if you love me, feed my lambs (my children). And last but not least, Peter, if you love me take care of my people (caring for the welfare of God's people). Now, how we fulfill Jesus' request is by following the Holy Spirit's instruction, and in order to follow the Holy Spirit's instructions, we must cement our relationships with God.

Well now, hopefully after reading this book you should have absolutely no problem in recognizing who the Pharisees among us are, all one has to do is to look at the many examples that exist right here and now, and right before our eyes on a daily basis. Let's view some of these examples: 1.) Ministers whose sermons consist only of preaching, while eliminating the teaching aspects of delivering God's words as presented by His Son, Jesus The Christ. The results of such preaching styles means that many people, who after hearing these types of messages, exit from such churches with no idea of how to apply what they have heard to their lives in our day and time. Also, the ministers that deliver through this preaching style, actually knowingly or unknowingly, omit the amount of racial inclusion that factually exist in the bible, even though the bible is not a history book about race. In addition, these ministers fail to explain the cultures of the times of which they speak and they also fail to explain where the events that they preach about took place, as such places relate to today's geography. Without this pertinent information, one cannot gain the proper prospective of mankind's origin, or mankind's Godly purpose in life as this purpose relate to each of us, regardless of race or gender.

2). Ministers who do not fully explain the adverse treatment of women during biblical times, the type of treatment that went total against God's will; treatment that consisted of no rights, no voice in their respective communities and the type of treatment that presented no opportunities for financial gains to sustain themselves except through arranged marriages or prostitution. And, why do we read so much about the women of prostitution in the bible, yet so little about the men that made prostitution a thriving enterprise, as they do today! One must keep in mind the old saying that history is not so much about what is written, but what actually happened, and when we fail to fully explain actually what happened and why it happened, we fail to truly communicate and understand history, be it social history or biblical history. Also, when any society or persons in a society remain ignorant about their history, then both are destine to repeat it, and that is why we are still witnessing the Pharisees Among Us, we simply continue to repeat our negative history. 3). One can still find that many denominations are still to this day neglecting to follow Jesus' example of allowing women to proclaim the teaching of our Lord and Savior, Jesus The Christ. In other words, in some denominations women still cannot become ministers or rise to positions of authority within such denominations. 4). We see so called Christians who read the bible every single day, yet they neglect to learn the correct interpretations about what they read, who they read about, or, where the events that they read about in the bible took place. In other words, such Christians continue to reflect the spiritual comprehension of their ministers' weekly sermons. Also, there are many Christians living among us that wrongly continue to use the bible as their own personal book of judgment, and when they do, they turn the bible into an instrument for religious stoning, by stoning those people who look different from them by historically distorting their lives and or their contributions, or by judging those people who may have a different life style than theirs. It is these types of judgmental Christians who assume the role of God, and in the process, they continue to influence still others to do the same.

5). In addition, we have seen too many of our religious leaders, as well as our institutional scholars choose to remain silent about the correct interpretations of many of the verses in the bible, even though they themselves are well aware of the correct interpretations. When these leaders choose not to share with us their learned input which would fully explain the verses in question, they in turn allow the wrong perceptions to persist, and it is these distorted perceptions that have worked to the advantage of one race over another race, of one person over another person, of one religion over another religion and of one gender over the other gender.

6). We also witness in our day and time many political leaders that advocate as well as perpetuate social policies and agendas which creates conditions of poverty, homelessness which in turn bring about various illnesses in societies in which millions of people are without health insurance. However, such politicians feel that to correct these conditions would be to promote SOCIALISM, so instead of doing the Godly acts of correcting these conditions in our societies as did Jesus The Christ did many times over, they continue to demonstrate their pernicious actions, which never at any time were demonstrated in the bible by Jesus Christ. So the question remains, exactly whose examples are these politicians following when they move our poor, sick and homeless brethren out of our sights, in other words, eradicate them by sweeping our disadvantage brothers and sisters under some type of social carpet. Now, one would think that after thousands of years these same leaders would have learned from Jesus Christ's many GRACIOUS examples while He walked this very same earth. Nevertheless, when it come to addressing the social needs of those among us who are disadvantaged, well, THE PHARISEES ARE STILL AMONG US!!

MATHEW 23, VERSE 23

Woe to you, teachers of the law and Pharisees, you hypocrites! You give a tenth of your spices, mints, dills and cummin.

But you have neglected the more important matters of law, justice, mercy and faithfulness. You should have practiced the latter without neglecting the former......

THE END